Policing Matters

Policing and Psychology

Nicholas Blagden

Series editors

P A J Waddington

Martin Wright

$SAGE

LearningMatters

Los Angeles | London | New Delhi
Singapore | Washington DC

www.learningmatters.co.uk

Los Angeles | London | New Delhi
Singapore | Washington DC

www.learningmatters.co.uk

Learning Matters
An imprint of SAGE Publications Ltd
1 Oliver's Yard
55 City Road
London EC1Y 1SP

SAGE Publications Inc.
2455 Teller Road
Thousand Oaks, California 91320

SAGE Publications India Pvt Ltd
B 1/I 1 Mohan Cooperative Industrial Area
Mathura Road
New Delhi 110 044

SAGE Publications Asia-Pacific Pte Ltd
3 Church Street
#10–14 Samsung Hub
Singapore 049483

Library of Congress Control Number: 2011945607

British Library Cataloguing in Publication Data

A catalogue record for this book is available from
the British Library

ISBN: 978 0 85725 465 8
ISBN: 978 0 85725 833 5

Editor: Julia Morris
Development editor: Jennifer Clark
Copy-editor: Sue Edwards
Production controller: Chris Marke
Project management: Diana Chambers
Marketing manager: Zoe Seaton
Cover design: Toucan Designs
Typeset by: Kelly Winter
Printed by: TJ International Ltd, Padstow, Cornwall

MIX
Paper from
responsible sources
FSC   FSC® C013056

Contents

Acknowledgements

I would like to thank colleagues from Huddersfield University, Lincoln University and Nottingham Trent University. My experiences of training police officers contributed to some of the insights in this book and I would like to thank the cohorts of students I taught while at Huddersfield. I would also like to thank Jennifer Clark for staying patient with me and mum and Emily for additional proofreads. Any errors, of course, are mine alone.

This book is dedicated to my wonderful family, to mum, dad, my wife Emily and our beautiful boys, Dylan and Jake. I love you all and I'm blessed to have you all in my life.

1   Policing and psychology: an introduction

This book is written at a time of change and uncertainty within the police force: government cuts, recruitment freezes and demands for increased public satisfaction and targets mean that job demands and pressure are likely to increase. As police management has become more professional and organised, there has become a greater appreciation of the contribution psychology can make to various aspects of policing. Indeed, psychological research has been influential in police training, police officer recruitment and selection, understanding stress and burnout, as well as contributing to specialist areas such as offender profiling and hostage-taking incidents (Kapardis, 2010). Perhaps one of the most important areas in which psychology has had an impact is in police–public relations, for example interactions with the general public, victims and offenders. This has played a crucial role in police training, where police officers are taught important skills such as listening and communication, effective decision-making, conflict-resolution, stress awareness, and stereotype and prejudice formation (Reiser, 1982; Reiser and Klyver, 1987; Sprackman, 2000; Skolnick, 2008). This is important as Goldstein has noted that *complaints arising from police-citizen contacts account for much of the attention the police receive* (1994, p323).

Police work is thus influenced by a range of dynamic psychological factors and understanding these factors can help to inform various aspects of operational policing (Brewer and Wilson, 1995). The purpose of this book is to highlight some of the crucial ways in which psychology can be applied to policing. Psychology has been defined as the scientific study of the human mind and behaviour and is regulated in the UK by the British Psychological Society (BPS, 2011). As psychology is concerned with the mind and behaviour, its relevance to policing is obvious. For example, psychological processes are evident every time a police officer interacts with a victim, member of the public or an offender. Similarly, psychological processes can be noted when using interview skills, for example when undertaking an investigative or cognitive interview or when the police request the assistance of a crime profiler. Given that psychology and psychological research are focused on mind and behaviour, it is little wonder that psychologists are increasingly interested in crime, criminals, criminal justice and rehabilitation (Reiser, 1982).

> ### PRACTICAL TASK
>
> *Think about the different ways in which psychology can be applied to policing, then compile a list of all the aspects of police work that are influenced by, or involve psychology to some degree.*

Police work and psychology

Sir Robert Peel was instrumental in creating and introducing the Metropolitan Police Force, with his initial aims for the modern police service still influential today. The police service is today governed by a tripartite system that was set up by the Police Act 1964. This Act outlined clear roles and responsibilities for the Home Secretary, the Police Authority (or committee as it was known at the time) and the Chief Constable. The purpose of this tripartite system was to ensure that there is no direct political interference in operational policing, while at the same time ensuring that the police were accountable, effective and efficient in their service (Blake et al., 2010). Blake et al. (2010, p15) highlight that the current aims of the police service are as follows.

- To uphold the law fairly and firmly.

- To prevent crime.

- To pursue and bring to justice those who break the law.

- To keep the Queen's peace.

- To protect, help and reassure the community.

- To be seen to do all things with integrity, common sense and sound judgement.

There are aspects of psychology that are applicable to all of the modern aims of policing. Indeed, the application of psychology to policing is nothing new and some have noted that the profession of 'police psychology' was born at the National Symposium on Police Psychological Services, which was held by the USA's Federal Bureau of Investigation (FBI) in 1984 (Bartol, 1996). However, some suggest that it was much earlier than that, citing that Martin Reiser was the first person to be employed as a police psychologist in 1968. However, it may have been in Europe where the origins of policing and psychology lay. It has been suggested that psychologists were used as early as 1919 in Germany and that, in 1966, Munich's police department had a full-time police psychologist employed to train police officers in various patrol-related issues (Bartol, 1996). However, the fit between psychology and policing has not always been an easy one and scepticism still remains between psychologists and police officers. The police have had a tendency to view psychologists as 'fuzzy-headed', not grounded in reality, 'cloud nine' thinkers and 'do-gooders', while psychologists have viewed the police as 'insensitive' and preferring brawn over brains (Ainsworth, 2002). Police perceptions may, in part, also be mediated by public views, which still tend to be that psychology is unscientific (Lilienfield, 2011).

There is now a growing mutual respect between the two disciplines, with psychology being recognised as extremely helpful in aiding police officers to understand and explain various phenomena related to police practice. Indeed, over the past two decades there has been a sustained increase in research on police psychology, which has even led to it being recognised by the American Psychology Association (APA) as a proficiency in professional psychology (Aumiller and Corey, 2007; Snook et al., 2009). Psychologists and psychological services employed by the police authorities, particularly in the UK, still remain low. There are psychologists who offer counselling services to the police and who are consulted in serious crime cases or for expertise in profiling. There is also the emergence of 'behavioural investigative advisers' (BIAs), who provide support for the investigation of serious crimes, including risk assessment, case linkage, interview strategy and cold case reviews (NPIA, 2011). However, while BIAs are becoming routine in serious crime cases, there are only five employed full time with over thirty who are consulted externally (NPIA, 2011).

In the USA the profession of police psychology is much better known, with many more full-time police psychologists employed. Their roles are also varied and diverse, and are not just based around criminal profiling and serious crimes. Scrivner (1994) found that police psychologists were employed more for their mental health services (e.g. counselling and 'well-being' training) and evaluations. Bartol (1996) found that police psychologists spent most of their time on screening (i.e. police officer recruitment) and counselling, with only 10 per cent on operational activities such as profiling, hostage negotiation and so on. Research also suggests that, in the USA, around 30–50 per cent of police departments use psychological services for training purposes and 10–30 per cent for assistance in investigations (Snook et al., 2009).

Although this book is concerned with police psychology, its main aim is to explore the different and practical ways in which psychology can be applied and have utility for policing practice. The book is thus centred on applying psychological theory to practice and, through understanding the various psychological concepts covered in this book, students and officers will be equipped with knowledge that will be relevant to their work and could enhance their performance.

Structure of the book

This book draws on a range of psychological theories, concepts and research to explore the relevance of psychology to modern-day policing. The book focuses on issues that are relevant to policing practice and that will be of interest to serving police officers, trainee officers and students with an interest in policing and psychology. There is a focus on issues that have direct implications for policing practice, such as communication skills, interacting with victims, coping with stress and burnout and the process of forming stereotypes and attributions. It also considers the evidence for criminal profiling and investigative psychology and the psychological explanations of crime and criminal behaviour. The book's chapters focus on the following areas.

In Chapter 2 the focus is on psychological theories of crime and criminal behaviour. An understanding of these theories will bolster knowledge on why certain people commit crimes. The theories that are explored are 'psycho-biological', which asks the question of whether crime is biologically or genetically driven. 'Attachment' theories focus on our early developmental experiences, particularly those with our parents or early care givers.

'Personality' theories as applied to criminal behaviour have attempted to uncover which personality types are likely to be more criminogenic and this chapter also explores whether there is a 'police personality'. The chapter also considers cognitive theories, which would suggest that crime occurs due to thinking errors or faulty decisions. Each of the theories discussed is linked to policing and police work.

Chapter 3 focuses on stereotypes, attributions and prejudice, and how they can affect police work. It explores how we formulate stereotypes and how they can lead to prejudice. It also explores how we make attributions about behaviour and how prone to error these can be.

Chapter 4 focuses on the importance of communication, interpersonal and interviewing skills in policing. It outlines the process of investigative interviews and critically discusses the skills needed for effective interviews with offenders and victims.

Chapter 5 focuses on investigative psychology and criminal profiling, and discusses the merits and myths of offender profiling.

Chapter 6 focuses on victims of crime and the impact of victimisation on individuals. This is a crucially important chapter given that there is great focus within police authorities on victim satisfaction and a recognition that victims are key stakeholders in the criminal justice system.

Chapter 7 explores the issues of stress and burnout in police officers. It considers what stress is and offers effective ways of coping with stress, both in general and applied to policing.

Chapter 8 offers a brief concluding summary.

REFERENCES

Ainsworth, PB (2002) *Psychology and Policing*. Cullompton: Willan.

Aumiller, GS and Corey, D (2007) Defining the Field of Police Psychology: Core domains and proficiencies. *Journal of Police and Criminal Psychology*, 22(2): 65–76.

Bartol, CR (1996) Police Psychology: Then, now, and beyond. *Criminal Justice and Behavior*, 23: 70–89.

Blake, C, Sheldon, B and Williams, P (2010) *Policing and Criminal Justice*. Exeter: Learning Matters.

BPS (British Psychological Society) (2011) Psychology and the Public. Online at www.bps.org.uk/psychology-public/psychology-and-public (accessed 2 February 2011).

Brewer, N and Wilson, C (eds) (1995) *Psychology and Policing*. Hillsdale, NJ: Lawrence Erlbaum.

Goldstein, H (1994) Controlling and Reviewing Police–Citizen Contact, in Barker, T and Carter, DL (eds) *Police Deviance*. Cincinnati, OH: Anderson.

Kapardis, A (2010) *Psychology and Law: A critical introduction.* Cambridge: Cambridge University Press.

Lilienfield, SO (2011) Public Skepticism of Psychology: Why many people perceive the study of human behaviour as unscientific. *American Psychologist*, 64(8): 644–58.

NPIA (National Policing Improvement Agency) (2011) Behavioural Investigative Advisors. Online at www.npia.police.uk/en/6852.htm (accessed 1 April 2011).

Reiser, M (1982) *Police Psychology: Collected papers.* Los Angeles, CA: LEHI.

Reiser, M and Klyver, N (1987) Consulting with the Police, in Weiner, IB and Hess, HK (eds) *Handbook of Forensic Psychology.* Chichester: John Wiley.

Scrivner, EM (1994) *The Role of Police Psychology in Controlling Excessive Force*. Washington, DC: National Institute of Justice.

Skolnick, J (2008) Enduring Issues of Police Culture and Demographics. *Policing and Society*, 18(1): 34–45.

Snook, B, Doan, B, Cullen, RM, Kavanagh, JM and Eastwood, J (2009) Publication and Research Trends in Police Psychology: A review of five forensic psychology journals. *Journal of Police and Criminal Psychology*, 24. 45–50.

Sprackman, P (2000) *Helping People Cope with Crime.* London: Hodder.

USEFUL WEBSITES

www.apa.org/ed/graduate/specialize/police.aspx – American Psychological Association, Public Description of Police Psychology

www.bps.org.uk/psychology-public/psychology-and-public – British Psychological Society, Psychology and the Public

www.i-psy.com – Centre for Investigative Psychology

www.npia.police.uk – National Policing Improvement Agency

www.npia.police.uk/en/6852.htm – NPIA information on behavioural investigative advisers (BIAs)

2 Psychological theories of crime and criminal behaviour

CHAPTER OBJECTIVES

By the end of this chapter you should be able to:

- understand some of the main psychological theories of crime and criminal behaviour;
- apply these theories to case studies and real-world policing examples;
- think critically about psychological theories of crime and their application to criminal behaviour.

LINKS TO STANDARDS

This chapter provides opportunities for links with the following Skills for Justice, National Occupational Standards (NOS) for Policing and Law Enforcement 2008.

AE1 Maintain and develop your knowledge, skills and competence.
HA2 Manage your own resources and professional development.
HF15 Provide information to support decision making.

With the introduction of the Qualification and Credit Framework (QCF), it is likely that the term 'National Occupational Standards' will change. At the time of writing, it is not clear what the new title will be, although it is known that some organisations will use the term 'QCF assessment units'.

Links to current NOS are provided at the start of each chapter; however, it should be noted that these are currently subject to review and it is recommended that you visit the Skills for Justice website to check the currency of all the NOS provided: www.skillsforjustice-nosfinder.com.

Introduction

Why people commit crime is something that academics and practitioners have tried to explain for many years. This chapter explores some of the main psychological theories that can help explain and predict why some people commit crime and others do not. The chapter aims to provide an in-depth summary of some of the key theories, including psycho-biological, social and cognitive-behavioural approaches. Through an understanding of these theories students, particularly those pursuing careers within law enforcement agencies, will gain an insight into the many factors that influence criminal behaviour. An understanding of these theories will broaden students' and trainee police officers' perceptions on what (if anything concrete) causes offending behaviour.

Psycho-biological theories

In the broad context of the nature/nurture debate, biological and psycho-biological theories favour the 'nature' explanations of criminal behaviour. Such theories suggest that there is something biologically pathological within the individual that leads to criminality, rather than their criminal behaviour resulting from environmental factors such as social deprivation, injustice or inequality. While early biological theories have been largely discredited, the advent of new technology, and particularly the proliferation of psycho-logical research using functional magnetic resonance imaging (fMRI) to study brain activity and structure, has led to a resurgence in biologically orientated explanations of offending. According to Raine (2004) genetic and biological factors play an equal, if not greater, role in the causation of criminal behaviour in comparison to social factors. However, let us first consider some of the early and later biological explanations of crime and criminal behaviour.

Cesare Lombroso (1876) probably provided one of the most famous early examples of a biological explanation of crime. Lombroso believed that criminals represented a form of degeneracy and that they were atavistic – a form of genetic throwback to an earlier form of evolution. For instance, Lombroso asserted that sloping foreheads, long arms, receding chins and unusually shaped ears were all physical characteristics of criminals (Lilly et al., 1995). He claimed that murderers had thick curly hair, strong jaws and bloodshot eyes, while sex offenders had slanting eyes, lots of hair and projecting ears. Lombroso's work is highly discredited for many reasons, such as not using control groups and using populations with a high presence of mental abnormality and dysfunction.

William Sheldon (1942) suggested that body shape was associated with personality type and outlined different body types, as follows.

- **Ectomorph** – tall, thin, restrained = introverted.

- **Mesomorph** – muscular, strong, triangular (V-shaped back) = aggressive and adventurous.

- **Endomorph** – large and heavy = sociable and relaxed.

Sheldon (1942) developed his theory after studying a large sample of males in a rehabili-tation institution and rated the body types of offenders according to the three groups (see

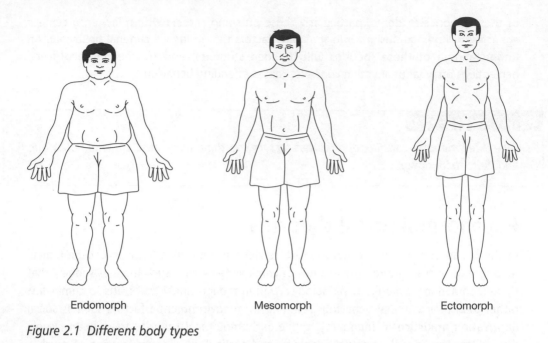

Endomorph   Mesomorph   Ectomorph

Figure 2.1 Different body types

Figure 2.1). He found a large number of mesomorphs, some endomorphs and very few ectomorphs in the institutional setting (Harrower, 1998). A similar study by Glueck and Glueck (1956) found that, compared to their control group, there were twice as many mesomorphs in the delinquent population. However, such theories have been heavily criticised with one criticism being the high probability that stereotyping (see Chapter 3) could be implicated in these findings. For instance, if the police or courts believe that criminals are a certain body shape, this may influence their decisions concerning arrests and convictions of individuals (Harrower, 1998). As we shall see in Chapter 3, we all make judgements about people on first impressions and it could be that the over-representation was due to people 'looking like criminals' or having faces that 'do not fit'.

In the 1960s a shift began from physical characteristics to the physiological characteristics linked to criminal behaviour. This period saw the emergence of a new explanation of crime through a focus on genetic abnormalities, most notably through the 'XYY syndrome'. This syndrome was a chromosomal abnormality with the individual possessing an extra Y chromosome. This syndrome is associated with low intelligence and above-average height. Studies in the 1960s and early 1970s asserted that there were more XYY males in prisons and hospitals and that they had a disproportionate propensity towards violent crime. It was argued that the presence of an extra Y chromosome resulted in the person having a severely disordered personality, making them more susceptible to criminal behaviour. It was further contended that XYY individuals (in institutional settings) were more likely to be hostile and violently aggressive (Price and Whatmore, 1967). However, the incidence of XYY in criminal populations (and general populations) is low. A critical Danish study (n=4591) found only 12 cases in the general public. While those individuals were more likely to be involved with crime (41.7 per cent XYY compared to 9.3 per cent XY), it was not violent crime (Harrower, 1998). The researchers suggested that their over-representation in prisons may be due to their low intelligence and height, coupled with the social reaction to those characteristics, causing criminality, for example their criminality could be influenced more by social reaction and their responses to that reaction (see, e.g., Becker, 1963).

Recently, there have been studies to suggest that genetics play a role in criminal behaviour, with several monoamine neurotransmitter genes associated with anti-social behaviour. One such gene – monoamine oxidase A (MAOA) (an enzyme that breaks down monoamines, e.g. serotonin and dopamine) – has been found to be implicated in aggressive and impulsive behaviour (Schug et al., 2010). For instance, a study by Caspi et al. (2002) found that maltreated children with a genotype conferring high levels of MAOA were less likely to become anti-social and violent in adolescence than maltreated children who had low levels of MAOA (Schug et al., 2010). However, we need to consider this critically. Crime and criminal behaviour depend on an interplay between many different factors and it is more complex than being dependent on particular genes. Indeed, Nilsson et al. (2006) found that MAOA did not predict criminality on its own, although they do suggest that a biopsychosocial model can contribute to understanding criminal behaviour, for example where biological factors are combined with unfavourable psychosocial conditions.

If genetics are implicated in crime (and the evidence is mixed), then does genetic inheritance play a causal role in offending? In other words, does crime tend to run in families and, if so, why? It has been found that individuals in families who are criminogenic or who associate with anti-social peers generally find themselves located in the nexus of risk factors for criminality. In other words, they are more likely to live in deprived areas, have poor education and suffer from relative deprivation. For instance, Rutter (1971) has found that risk factors for delinquency include family criminality, ineffective and inconsistent discipline, and anti-social development (and association with peers). However, it is very difficult to say whether this is due to genetics or environment. Biological studies cannot control for social context or environment. In statistical analysis we are always mindful to remember that correlation does not equal causation, so just because something is associated with criminality this does not mean it causes it (or even plays a major role in it). Studies that focus on genetics and families suggest that heritable factors may increase and influence criminal behaviour – but evidence is not conclusive.

Until recently much of the early biological research has been discredited or heavily criticised and, as a result, the favoured approach to explaining crime and criminal behaviour has been to focus on social factors, for example socio-economic area, poverty, relative deprivation, peer group or schooling. However, there has recently been a resurgence in biological explanations of some criminal groups. Raine (2004) has suggested that evidence for biological factors in crime is now overwhelming and cannot be ignored. In one study, Raine et al. (1997) found differences in brain function and activity in the brains of murderers when compared to controls. They found reduced glucose metabolism in the prefrontal cortex and abnormalities in the amygdala. Deficits in these regions of the brain are associated with impulsivity, loss of self-control and immaturity. Furthermore, abnormalities in the amygdala are associated with aggressive behaviour. These brain abnormalities may explain why some people turn to crime and others do not. Again, we need to be cautious of the findings of such studies; the sample used by Raine et al. (1997) was comparatively small and all the murderers were not guilty by reason of insanity (NGRI). However, murderers differ considerably in motivation and causation, and not all are criminally insane (far from it). In further studies, Raine (1996) found that violent and sexual offending can be traced to deficits in brain structure and function, while reduced brain grey matter in the prefrontal cortex was associated with anti-social personality disorder. However, it is unknown how many people have such abnormalities in the general public and yet lead offence-free lives.

There is also evidence that biological factors are implicated in antecedents associated with offending, most notably with psychopathy. Although debated, psychopathy is usually defined as a specific form of personality disorder characterised by deficits in affective and interpersonal functioning (Huss, 2009). Cleckley (1941) described psychopathy as a disorder in which individuals are unable to experience feelings of empathy, anxiety, remorse or guilt; they manipulate and exploit others and engage in risky behaviours to satisfy their own needs with little concern for the consequences. Psychopathy is a clinical construct measured using the PCL-R (psychopathy checklist revised) and is split into two factors: factor 1 is the interpersonal and affective domain (it includes factors such as superficial charm, manipulative behaviour and lack of empathy); factor 2 is the anti-social lifestyle/attitudes domain (it includes impulsivity, irresponsibility, early behavioural problems and a parasitic lifestyle). Salekin et al. (1996) found a significant relationship between psychopathy and general criminal recidivism, and an even larger relationship between violent recidivism and psychopathy. Hemphill et al. (1998) found the factor 2 domain a better predictor of general recidivism, but factors 1 and 2 predicted violent recidivism equally. Psychopathy has also been found to be predictive of sexual recidivism. Offenders with higher PCL-R scores commit more severe violent and sexual crimes (Huss, 2009).

It may be that a mix of genetic, environmental and social factors for some vulnerable children produces a higher probability of criminal behaviour. Schug et al. (2010) argue that gene–environment interactions are important in the development and progression of anti-social behaviour and criminality. This is noted by Popma and Raine (2006) in their explanation of social-push theory. This theory states that, when an anti-social child lacks the social factors that 'push' the child into anti-social behaviour, biological factors may be more likely to explain their behaviour. However, we must again be cautious about interpreting findings of biological explanations of crime and criminal behaviour. Rose (2004) contends that a child from an abusive environment with a particular genetic mutation may be more likely to become violent or abusive when they are older. The genetic mutation, however, is rare while the environment is common. Thus, Rose contends that, if we want to do something about this cycle, it is best to prevent any child (with or without such genes) from being abused.

Do you think criminals are born (nature) or made (nurture)?

Get a piece of paper and divide it in half; on one side write down the arguments for nature (criminals are born) and, on the other, those for nurture (criminals are made). Then visit http://news.bbc.co.uk/2/hi/programmes/if/4102371.stm and read the debate between Professor Adrian Raine and Professor Steven Rose on biology and crime.

Who do you agree with? Consider why this may be the case. We will reconsider this later after examining further psychological theories of crime.

Attachment

Attachment theory can be thought of as an integrative approach within psychology as it is influenced by different psychological perspectives – biological, social and evolutionary. Attachment theory was also originally derived, in part, from psychoanalytical traditions. Indeed, John Bowlby's (1969) original theory was concerned with maternal loss and subsequent personality development. For Bowlby the attachment system is created to regulate behaviour designed to obtain and maintain proximity to a preferred individual – the attachment figure. In Bowlby's (1946) study he collated and contrasted 44 case histories of juveniles who had committed theft with those of 44 children who had been referred to psychiatric services. Among the group of thieves he found an over-representation of certain psychological dispositions, including 'affectionless characters' (individuals who showed little shame, sense of responsibility or any normal affection) (Gadd and Jefferson, 2007). The 'affectionless characters' were the group most likely to reoffend, had few real friendships, found it difficult to foster meaningful relationships and felt lonely and isolated (Gadd and Jefferson, 2007). Bowlby (1946) found that this group had prolonged separations from their parents (although the focus was on the mother), or had an emotionally cold mother; that is, they suffered the emotional loss of their mothers. For Bowlby (1946) this led to a failure of the superego (which reflects the internalisation of standards, morals and customs learnt through parents and other socialising agents) to form adequately due to failure in the development of object-love (love of another).

Early attachment relationships, whether positive or negative, are considered to provide children with a template for the construction of their future relationships and their role in future relationships. The attachment system, part of the internal model concerning relationships, is based on components that include memories of attachment-related experiences, beliefs, expectations and attitudes about a relationship, and strategies and plans for achieving attachment goals (Rich, 2003). Individuals then differ in their attachment styles and these can affect their relationships with others. Mary Ainsworth was the first to derive a model of attachment style. Her model was based on her 'strange-situations test', which involved observing 12-month-olds under test conditions. The strange-situations test comprised five elements.

- Parent and child alone in room.
- Child explores environment with parent present.

- Stranger enters, talks to parent, interacts with child.

- Parent leaves the room quietly.

- Parent returns and comforts the child (20 minutes later).

It is through Ainsworth et al.'s (1978) observations that they came up with three categories of attachment – secure attachment, anxious-ambivalent insecure attachment, and anxious-avoidant insecure attachment.

- **Secure attachment** – children did not experience significant distress when the mother left. When the mother was present the child explored his or her surroundings freely and interacted with the stranger. Although maybe visibly upset when the mother left, the child was comforted by her return (Rich, 2003).

- **Anxious-ambivalent insecure attachment** – the child is anxious of exploring others in the presence of the mother. The child will be extremely distressed when he or she is left with the stranger and will often be hostile when the mother returns.

- **Anxious-avoidant insecure attachment** – children tend to avoid parents and care-givers. Although they may not reject attention from their mothers, they will not pursue it or seek it out. In adult life this attachment style can have serious ramifications, as these individuals often have difficulties forming intimate relationships and are perceived as emotionally cold.

Attachment styles are also associated with different types of offending behaviour. For instance, Ward et al. (1996) found that sex offenders were insecurely attached in their romantic relationships. Rapists tended to be dismissive in their attachment styles and so tended to hold more hostile views of women and offended in a more aggressive manner. Child sex offenders are more likely to be fearful or insecure in attachment style and this was also evident in their high social anxiety and poor social skills. They also viewed women and adult relationships as 'dangerous'. Rutter (1971) also found that failure to form an attachment bond to a primary caregiver was a significant factor in later-life delinquency. Furthermore, he found that delinquents separated from their mothers possessed 'affec-tionless characters'. Interestingly, Laub and Sampson (2006) found that attachment may play a role in persisting in and desisting from crime. They found that *the persistent offender seemed devoid of connective structures at each stage of the life-course, especially involving relationships that can provide informal social control and social support* (Laub and Sampson, 2006, p194).

Social learning and differential association

Albert Bandura's social learning theory emerged during the 1970s and is a product of a combination of behaviourism and cognitive psychology. The crux of social learning is that we learn directly from observing others, particularly if they are of high status. In social learning there is an actively 'cognitive' part in learning, for example through observing others, and you are more likely to copy behaviour that yields pleasurable responses (Newburn, 2007). One cognitive aspect incorporated in social learning is an individual's reflection upon personal experience, such as successes and failures, and using this internal process as a reinforcement or punishment (Bandura, 1977). Social learning was influenced by BF Skinner's operant conditioning theory, which stated that behaviour could be shaped by positive and negative reinforcement, as well as through punishment. Operant conditioning asserted that desired behaviour will increase when followed by positive reinforcement and decrease following punishment.

Social learning theory also includes a consideration of motivation (Newburn, 2007):

- **external reinforcement** (from environment);
- **vicarious reinforcement** (from observing others);
- **self-reinforcement** (as a result of taking pleasure or pride from one's own actions).

Criminal behaviour occurs through interaction with an individual's social environment. In such social settings consequences are attached to their behaviour that reinforce or punish deviant acts. If someone learns in an environment where deviant or criminal behaviour is reinforced or regarded highly, that individual is more likely to participate in crime and anti-social behaviour (Akers, 1985). This is exemplified in Edwin Sutherland's differential association theory, which states that behaviour is influenced by the norms of groups to which one belongs. Through learning and imitation from members of the group, individual behaviour is shaped. Becoming embroiled in criminality involves learning the attitudes and values that are associated with criminality (Hollin, 1992). Thus, differential association is criminal behaviour that is learned in association with others. Criminality reflects the 'definitions favourable to crime' in one's social environment.

Personality

Hans Eysenck's theory of personality is an attempt to combine biological, psychological and individual difference factors. While it is often seen as a general theory of crime, it is actually more specific and attempts to explain why some people fail to follow rules, become anti-social and turn to crime (Harrower, 1998). Eysenck (1998) believed that personality and crime were a product of biology and genetics, and used the same studies we looked at earlier as evidence for this. The basis of Eysenck's theory begins with classical conditioning – the child learns by association, which brings about a fear response to anti-social behaviour (because of punishment from parents and/or teachers). However, we are not all conditioned to the environment in the same way and Eysenck would argue that this 'conditionability' is due, in part, to genetic inheritance (Hollin, 1992).

Eysenck and Eysenck (1991) put forward a three-factor model of personality. The traits in this model were extraversion–introversion, neuroticism–stability and psychotism. Extraverts (E) are more likely to act on impulse and seek out excitement; they tend to *crave excitement [while acting] on the spur of the moment* (Eysenck and Eysenck, 1991, p4). The introvert (I) tends to be a person who is reserved, quiet and cautious (Bartol and Bartol, 2004) and so is unlikely to become a criminal. Neurotics (N) tend to be suffering from high levels of anxiety and depression, and have strong emotional reactions. Those who are towards the stable end of the dimension tend to condition to the environment well and do not display overly emotional reactions. The last dimension in Eysenck and Eysenck's

(1991) three-factor model, psychoticism (P), is separate from the other two personality dimensions. Those who are found to be 'high P' tend to be emotionally cold, impersonal, poor perspective takers and more likely to participate in anti-social behaviour (Williams et al., 2010). Figure 2.2 shows Eysenck and Eysenck's (1991) personality circle, which shows the dimensions of a person's personality. Where the persona is plotted between the dimensions of neurotic–emotionally stable and introverted–extraverted will determine a person's personality, so someone who is emotionally stable and extraverted is likely to be sociable and easy-going.

So what is the relationship between personality and crime? Eysenck argued that, in terms of the central nervous system (CNS), introverts are cortically over-aroused and so they will behave in ways to minimise arousal, while extraverts are cortically under-aroused and so will seek out sensation because they are under-aroused. It is predicted that stable introverts (low E, low N) will condition best, stable extraverts (low N, high E) and neurotic introverts (high N, low E) will be in the middle, while neurotic extraverts (high N, high E) will condition least well (Hollin, 1992). If offending is linked to personality and if

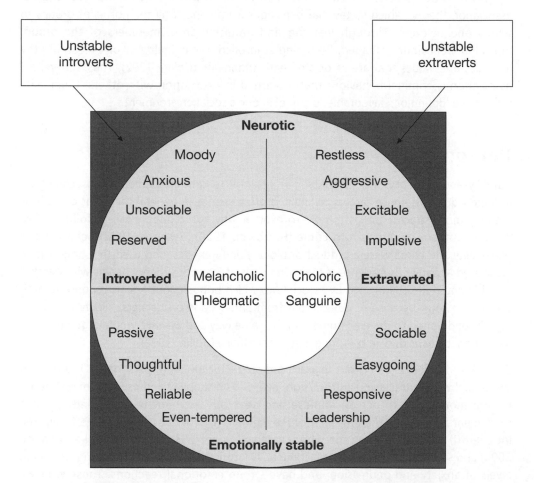

Figure 2.2 Eysenck and Eysenck's personality circle (adapted from Eysenck and Eysenck, 1991, and Williams et al., 2010)

conditionability and socialisation are linked to control of anti-social behaviour, we would expect high N, high E personalities to be involved in crime (Hollin, 1992). High psychoticism (P) is a strong predictor of criminality because of associated factors, such as being emotionally cold, unempathetic, anti-social, tough-minded and egocentric (Eysenck, 1998). It is important to note that personality traits are not the only things that influence behaviour and there is a good deal of research that would argue that they are not that strong at predicting how we will behave in certain situations (Williams et al., 2010).

A police personality?

Do police officers have a certain type of personality? Does being a police officer affect an individual's personality? These are some of the questions that have been investigated with regard to policing and personality. The characteristics sometimes attributed to police personalities are those of machismo, cynicism, authoritarianism, aggressiveness and bravery (Twersky-Glasner, 2005). However, are these really the personality attributes that police recruiters look for? New police recruits will bring with them their own personalities, and the recruitment process and demands of the job will select those with the most appropriate personality for police work. This is important as policing can be highly stressful and can be an emotionally taxing occupation. In the USA, police departments use a battery of psychological tests, including personality tests, in order to 'screen out' unsuitable applicants. It has been found that the successful police recruits *do not* display traits of impulsivity, hostility, undue aggression, anti-social tendencies, potential for drug/alcohol abuse, social introversion and paranoia (Twersky-Glasner, 2005). It has been found that 15 per cent of potential police recruits are screened out through the use of personality tests (Bartol, 1996). Research has also shown that there are significant differences between unsuccessful police recruits and police officers, including police officers being more assertive and having more self-confidence, more functional intelligence and better impulse control (Twersky-Glasner, 2005). This supports other research cited in Winter (2003), which has found that the police are not a maladjusted group and may even be a superior subset of the population. However, other research does not support the latter assertion and it has been found that police officers with many years' service are more prone to stress, burnout and violence (Blau, 1994; Gershon et al., 2009).

If the recruitment process screens out the unsuitable police officers, it is reasonable to assume that many police officers will have similar personality constructs. Is it, then, something about the nature of police work that can shape or change personality into the stereotypical 'police personality'? According to Kroes (1985), it is rare that a police officer does not experience some negative personality change due to their years on the force. Blau (1994) has found that police officers, even after two years, can experience changes to their personality and attitudes. They have been found to show more anxiety, stress, alcohol-abuse vulnerability and more negative adjustment, which would have screened them out in the recruitment process. In a study of personality patterns in British police officers, which compared groups of experienced police officers and new recruits, it was found that new recruits tended to be higher in extraversion, venturesome and impulsive, whereas experienced officers were controlled and had fewer empathetic responses (Gudjonsson and Adlam, 1985).

As the personality of police officers appears to change throughout their working lives, it calls into question the use of personality tests in the recruitment process as they cannot predict how years of service will affect or shape personalities (Ainsworth, 2002). Indeed, what happens to officers during their careers continues to shape their personalities, so it would appear that job-related experiences contribute to the police personality (Twersky-Glasner, 2005). Although there is evidence to suggest that 'police personalities' may not be automatically negative, Evans et al. (1992) have found that experienced officers actually display less anxiety than new officers. It is therefore not conclusive as to whether years in the police service adversely affects officers' personalities or whether certain personality types are better suited for police work. It may be, however, that certain personality types are more drawn to police work than others, due to the appeals of policing.

REFLECTIVE TASK

- *Do criminals and police officers have different personalities? What personality traits would you expect a police officer and a criminal to have? Are there any similarities?*

- *Do you think personality theories can help explain behaviour? When answering this question think about how your personality has changed or stayed the same over the years. Are you the same person? Do you react to things in the same way?*

Cognitive-behavioural theories

The dominant and currently most influential psychological approach in explaining criminal behaviour, and thus important for police work, is the social-cognitive paradigm, or what can loosely be termed the cognitive-behavioural approach. An important concept within the social-cognitive paradigm for understanding offending behaviour is the 'schema'. Schemas (or schemata) are cognitive structures that help us make sense of our experience and help us anticipate future events (because schemas develop from early learning experiences). Schemas operate at a deeper level of cognition; they represent the cognitive structures that organise a person's experience (DeRubeis et al., 2001). Put simply, criminal behaviour is the result of an individual's beliefs, attitudes and values that are shaped by life experiences and affect future behaviour. Schemas guide our thought processes and thinking and affect our decision making, also forming the basis for individual instances of bias or distortion (DeRubeis et al., 2001). When a schema is identified it can usually be stated in the form of 'if–then' propositions, for example *if I do not succeed in everything, then I am a failure* (DeRubeis et al., 2001).

Schemas develop from a young age and allow us to make predictions about the world, for example 'generally people are hostile, threatening, kind etc.' They guide the interpretation of social information, goals and motivations in social settings, and also impact on our moral judgements, the perspectives we take and our moral reasoning development (Palmer, 2007). Early socialisation and learning experiences play an important role in developing healthy and maladaptive schemas, with parents and other social agents playing a vital role. Many of these early socialisation factors are implicated in later-life criminality, with many parental factors associated with the development of aggressive and criminal behaviour. For instance, it has been found that harsh parental disciplinary practices are associated with children developing hostile schemas. Harsh discipline and neglect from mothers are also associated with high levels of aggression in young children (Palmer, 2007). This has led Palmer (2007) to argue that children who experience harsh and neglectful parenting are at risk of developing offence-supportive cognitions and hostile schemas, which will affect how children interpret social cues and situations. People with hostile schemas can interpret the most neutral social cues or experiences as threatening or hostile and so are more likely to respond aggressively in those situations.

A further important concept for social-cognitive theories, particularly for offending behaviour and rehabilitation, is 'cognitive distortions'. Murphy (1990) argues that cognitive distortions are *self-statements made by offenders that allow them to deny, minimise, justify and rationalise their behaviour* (Murphy 1990, p332). Offenders' rationalisations and justifications are seen as representing their world view or attitudes towards certain people and are considered to play a causal role in offending (though this point is debated). Social-cognitive theorists, such as those who advocate schema models, would suggest that cognitive distortions arise from a cognitive schema related to the offender's world view, attitudes and beliefs about self and the victim (Yates, 2009). For instance, if a child molester holds the schema 'children are sexually provocative and can give consent', they may interpret benign behaviour from the child (e.g. smiling, sitting on one's knee) as an indicator of sexual interest and construe that sex with the child is reciprocal (Ward and Keenan, 1999; Yates, 2009). Much of the work in offending behaviour programmes is focused on correcting these disordered or maladaptive thinking patterns.

The thinking patterns outlined can be considered important as they may reflect an offender's beliefs or attitudes, which may drive an individual's offending. The following case study is an extract from an offence account from a research interview that focused on participants' reasons for maintenance and overcoming denial of their offences (see, e.g., Blagden et al., 2011). The case study is from an offender named Harvey (real name changed) who is a 30-year-old man and who is currently serving six years for the aggravated rape of his sister-in-law.

CASE STUDY

We had a close relationship [him and the victim] anyway, a friendship relationship, but she was a very attractive girl . . . I think I had thoughts, illicit thoughts about her and I think I dwelt on those thoughts erm through watching the pornography and getting a more depraved thought of what sex is, more and more thoughts built up about her . . . So it's a build-up of the thoughts that made me cross over from fantasy [to] reality. I had a stressful kind of job; I was just sacked from my job a week before the offence . . . So that was a contributing factor, I don't know how much, in terms of pushing me from fantasy to reality.

[I said] I'd slept with her but I didn't rape her it's consensual. There'd been bits in the past where she'd flirted with me and stuff, so I knew there was a bit of grounds to say she was a player and come onto me before . . .

. . . the reason I denied it was because I couldn't believe I'd done it, it was totally out of character – no way. Number two, I don't think anybody else could believe I'd done it.

Although he is admitting the offence, there are elements of his offence account that would be classed as containing cognitive distortions. It can be noted that he externalises blame for the offence by claiming that his loss of employment contributed to his offending behaviour. He also attempts to excuse and rationalise his behaviour by contending that the offence occurred because of his thoughts at the time, which had become preoccupied with a more 'depraved' view of sex. Through accounting for his behaviour in such a way, he is able to divorce himself from the act and not see his behaviour as part of him. This can be noted when retrospectively accounting for why he denied and minimised it, because he could not believe he had done it and that it was 'out of character'.

There is a large body of psychological research that focuses on the 'decision-making' processes of offenders. Yochelson and Samenow (1976) claimed to have identified the 'thinking errors' that characterised *all* criminals (see Table 2.1). They found a number of flawed ways of thinking that were common among criminals. While most people are capable of making rational decisions, the 'criminal personality' features a range of faulty thinking patterns.

Table 2.1 Yochelson and Samenow's thinking errors in criminal personalities

	Character traits	Automatic thinking errors	Errors associated with criminal acts
Types of error	Pervasive fearfulness Feelings of worthlessness Need for power and control Perfectionism	Lying and denials Poor decision making Lack of trust Secretiveness Failure to understand others' positions Failure to assume obligations Fantasies of anti-social behaviour	Corrosion of internal and external deterrents Super optimism

Source: Adapted from Newburn (2007, p158).

REFLECTIVE TASK

Think for a minute about some of the 'thinking errors' found in the 'criminal personality' – what is striking about them? How do they relate to 'normal' people in the general public?

Perhaps the most striking thing about the factors in the 'criminal personality' is that many of them can be found in people who are non-criminogenic and who lead offence-free lives. We all make poor decisions from time to time, fail to understand other people's positions, lie or deny (something we do on a daily basis). It is important to think critically before we pathologise certain characteristics. Indeed, a criticism of 'psychological positivistic research' (research that suggests that the cause of crime can be discovered through scientific investigation) is that it works from the endpoint. It draws inferences from a small population of individuals who have been convicted of offences and generalises them to the larger population. It does not account for those who may have these traits and do not commit crime. It could be that criminals have these traits in extremes, which, coupled with problematic backgrounds, could lead to poorer self-control. Self-control has been defined as *the tendency to avoid acts whose long-term costs exceed their momentary advantages* (Hirschi and Gottfredson, 1994, p3). Hirschi (2004) contends that people who commit delinquent acts or crimes are concerned with immediate gratification of desires. Those with low self-control have a 'here and now' orientation and so do not consider the future, whereas people with high self-control defer gratification. In short, people with low self-control tend to commit crime and delinquency because they are impulsive, risk-seeking, insensitive and short-sighted.

CASE STUDY

Josh is 14 and is already well known to the police for acts of anti-social behaviour in his community and for thefts from the local shop. His anti-social behaviour has resulted in Josh having an 'acceptable behaviour contract' for which he has had to pledge that he will no longer commit anti-social behaviour in his area. Failure to comply with this will mean he will be issued with an anti-social behaviour order (ASBO). Josh is frequently absent from school and, when he is there, he is disruptive and aggressive. He has been involved in numerous fights and he is warned that his continued behaviour will result in his permanent exclusion from school. Social services are involved with Josh and are concerned with his home life. Josh's father has been arrested numerous times for domestic violence against Josh's mother; however, the mother does not press charges. It is highly likely that Josh has witnessed domestic assault and social services also believe that he may have been a victim as well. Josh's father has a criminal record for violence and drug offences. The school has attempted to involve Josh's parents in his education, but they have refused to be involved. They seem to have little interest in his education or his behaviour. Social services, who have visited the mother, have described her as having a distant relationship with her son and as 'emotionally cold'.

The above case study could reflect, to some extent, many individuals you may come across in your role as a police officer. How do the theories in this chapter apply to this case?

REFLECTIVE TASK

We have now considered a range of psychological theories, some biologically orientated, some integrated in their perspective and others based on social cognition. Think again about whether crime is more nature or nurture. Which do you favour? Write a short paragraph as to why you take a particular position.

C H A P T E R   S U M M A R Y

This chapter has outlined some of the key psychological theories for understanding crime and criminal behaviour, which have offered an insight into the complex and diverse explanations of criminal behaviour. These theories can all have an impact on policing, as police work involves spending a great deal of time with those committing criminal acts. Through understanding these theories, we can better understand the complexities of crime. This can help guard against making stereotypical assumptions about certain criminals and criminal types, and instead can help one gain an informed view of crime and the individual causes of crime.

Although none of these theories gives us a complete picture or explanation of why some people commit certain types of crime, they can nevertheless give students and those working in the police a rounded understanding of some of the major factors associated with criminal behaviour. The theories covered in this chapter have evaluated the biological and genetic, attachment and social-cognitive explanations of criminal behaviour. Although not conclusive, it is clear that a range of biological, social and cognitive structures are implicated and play a role in offending behaviour. Although not considered in detail here, we cannot ignore social environment. Farrington and Hawkins (1991) conducted a longitudinal study of working-class boys to see which boys turned to crime. They found that poor income, large families, parental criminality and poor child-rearing techniques were important contributory factors in later-life criminality. It is little wonder, then, that many offenders find themselves in a nexus of social exclusion, disadvantage and negative life events.

FURTHER READING

Eysenck, HJ (1998) Personality and Crime, in Millon, T, Simonsen, E, Birket-Smith, M and Davis, RD (eds) *Psychopathy: Antisocial behaviour, criminal, and violent behaviour.* London: Guilford Press.

Gannon, TA, Ward, T, Beech, AR and Fisher, D (eds) (2007) *Aggressive Offenders' Cognition,* Chichester: John Wiley.

Raine, A, Buchsbaum, M and Lacasse, L (1997) Brain Abnormalities in Murderers Indicated by Positron Emission Tomography. *Biological Psychiatry,* 42(6): 495–508.

Rich, P (2003) *Attachment and Sexual Offending: Understanding and applying attachment theory to the treatment of juvenile sexual offenders.* Chicester: John Wiley.

REFERENCES

Ainsworth, MDS, Blehar, MC, Waters, E and Wall, S (1978) *Patterns of Attachment.* Hillsdale, NJ: Lawrence Erlbaum.

Ainsworth, PB (2002) *Psychology and Policing.* Cullompton: Willan.

Akers, RL (1985) *Deviant Behaviour: A social learning approach.* Belmont, CA: Wadsworth.

Bandura, A (1977) *Social Learning Theory.* Englewood Cliffs, NJ: Prentice Hall.

Bartol, CR (1996) Police Psychology: Then, now and beyond. *Criminal Justice and Behavior*, 23: 70–89.

Bartol, CR and Bartol, AM (2004) *Introduction to Forensic Psychology.* London: Sage.

Becker, H (1963) *Outsiders: Studies in the sociology of deviance.* New York: Free Press.

Blagden, N, Winder, B, Thorne, T and Gregson, M (2011) 'No-one in the World Would Ever Wanna Speak to me Again': An interpretative phenomenological analysis into convicted sexual offenders' accounts and experiences of maintaining and leaving denial. *Psychology, Crime and Law*, 17(1): 563–85.

Blau, TH (1994) *Psychological Services for Law Enforcement.* New York: John Wiley.

Bowlby, J (1946) *Forty-four Juvenile Thieves.* London: Baillière, Tindall and Cox.

Bowlby, J (1969) *Attachment and Loss, volume I: Attachment*. New York: Basic Books.

Caspi, A, McClay, J, Moffitt, TE, Mill, J, Martin, J, Craig, IW, Taylor, A and Poulton, R (2002) Role of Genotype in the Cycle of Violence in Maltreated Children. *Science*, 297(5582): 851–4.

Cleckley, HM (1941) *The Mask of Sanity*. St Louis, MO: Mosby.

DeRubeis, RJ, Tang, TZ and Beck, AT (2001) Cognitive Therapy, in Dobson, KS (ed.) *Handbook of Cognitive Behavioural Therapies.* London: Guilford Press.

Evans, BJ, Coman, GJ and Stanley, RO (1992) The Police Personality: Type A behaviour and trait anxiety. *Journal of Criminal Justice*, 20(5): 429–41.

Eysenck, HJ (1998) Personality and Crime, in Millon, T, Simonsen, E, Birket-Smith, M and Davis, RD (eds) *Psychopathy: Antisocial behaviour, criminal, and violent behaviour.* London: Guilford Press.

Eysenck, HJ and Eysenck, SJ (1991) *Manual of the Eysenck Personality Scales (EPS Adult): Comprising the EPQ-Revised (EPQ-R), EPQ-R short scale, Impulsiveness (IVE) questionnaire*. London: Hodder and Stoughton.

Farrington, DP and Hawkins, JD (1991) Predicting Participation, Early Onset, and Later Persistence in Officially Recorded Offending. *Criminal Behaviour and Mental Health*, 1: 1–33.

Gadd, D and Jefferson, T (2007) *Psychosocial Criminology.* London: Sage.

Gershon, R, Barocas, B, Canton, AN, Li, X and Vlahov, D (2009) Mental, Physical, and Behavioral Outcomes Associated with Perceived Work Stress in Police Officers. *Criminal Justice and Behavior*, 36: 275–89.

Glueck, S and Glueck, E (1956) *Physique and Delinquency*. New York: Harper.

Gudjonsson, GH and Adlam, K (1985) Occupational Stressors among British Police Officers. *Police Journal*, 58: 73–85.

Hemphill, JF, Hare, R and Wong, S (1998) Psychopathy and Recidivism: A review. *Legal and Criminological Psychology*, 3(1): 139–70.

Hirschi, T (2004) Self-control and Crime, in Baumeister, RF and Vohs, KD (eds) *Handbook of Self-regulation*. London: Guilford Press.

Hirschi, T and Gottfredson, M (1994) The Generality of Deviance, in Hirschi, T and Gottfredson, M (eds) *The Generality of Deviance*. New Brunswick, NJ: Transaction.

Harrower, J (1998) *Applying Psychology to Crime*. London: Hodder Education.

Hollin, CR (1992) *Criminal Behaviour: A psychological approach to explanation and prevention*. London: Farmer Press.

Huss, MT (2009) *Forensic Psychology: Research, clinical practice and applications*. Chichester: John Wiley.

Kroes, WH (1985) *Society's Victim: The police officer*. Springfield, IL: Thomas.

Laub, JH and Sampson, RJ (2006) *Shared Beginnings, Divergent Lives: Delinquent boys to age 70*. London: Harvard University Press.

Lilly, RJ, Cullen, FT and Ball, RA (1995) *Criminological Theory: Context and consequences*. London: Sage.

Lombroso, C (1876) *Criminal Man*. New York: GP Puttman.

Murphy, WD (1990) Assessment and Modification of Cognitive Distortions in Sex Offenders, in Marshall, WL, Laws, RD and Barbaree, H (eds) *Handbook of Sexual Assault: Issues, theory and treatment of the offender*. New York: Plenum.

Newburn, T (2007) *Criminology*. Cullompton: Willan.

Nilsson, KW, Sjoberg, RL, Damberg, M, Leppert, J, Ohrvik, J, Alm, PO, Lindstrom, L and Oreland, L (2006) Role of Monoamine Oxidase A Genotype and Psychosocial Factors in Male Adolescent Criminal Activity. *Biological Psychiatry*, 59(2): 121–7.

Palmer, EJ (2007) Moral Cognition and Aggression, in Gannon, TA, Ward, T, Beech, A and Fisher, D (eds) *Aggressive Offenders' Cognition: Theory, research and practice*. Chichester: John Wiley.

Popma, A and Raine, A (2006) Will Future Forensic Assessment be Neurobiologic? *Child and Adolescent Psychiatric Clinics of North America*, 15(2): 429–44.

Price, WH and Whatmore, PB (1967) Behaviour Disorders and Patterns of Crime among XYY Males Identified at a Maximum Security Hospital. *British Medical Journal*, 1: 533–6.

Raine, A (1996) Autonomic Nervous System Activity and Violence, in Stoff, DM and Cairns, RB (eds) *Aggression and Violence: Genetic, neurobiological and biosocial perspectives*. Mahwah, NJ: Erlbaum.

Raine, A (2004) 'Biological Key' to Unlocking Crime. Online at http://news.bbc.co.uk/1/hi/programmes/if/4102371.stm (accessed 1 February 2011).

Raine, A, Buchsbaum, M and Lacasse, L (1997) Brain Abnormalities in Murderers Indicated by Positron Emission Tomography. *Biological Psychiatry*, 42(6): 495–508.

Rich, P (2003) *Attachment and Sexual Offending: Understanding and applying attachment theory to the treatment of juvenile sexual offenders*. Chicester: John Wiley.

Rose, S (2004) Violence 'Not Detectable' by Brain Imaging. Online at http://news.bbc.co.uk/1/hi/programmes/if/4106217.stm (accessed 1 October 2010).

Rutter, M (1971) Parent–Child Separation: Psychological effects on the children. *Journal of Child Psychology and Psychiatry*, 12(4): 233–60.

Salekin, RT, Rogers, R and Sewell, KW (1996) A Review and Meta-analysis of the Psychopathy Checklist and Psychopathy Checklist-Revised: Predictive validity of dangerousness. *Clinical Psychology: Science and Practice*, 3(3): 203–15.

Schug, RA, Gao, Y, Glenn, AL, Peskin, M, Yang, Y and Raine, A (2010) The Developmental Evidence Base: Neurobiological research and forensic applications, in Towl, GJ and Crighton, DA (eds) *Forensic Psychology*. Chichester: Wiley- Blackwell.

Sheldon, WH (1942) *The Varieties of Temperament*. New York: Harper.

Twersky-Glasner, A (2005) Police Personality: What is it like and why are they like that? *Journal of Police and Criminal Psychology*, 20(1): 56–67.

Ward, T and Keenan, T (1999) Child Molesters' Implicit Theories. *Journal of Interpersonal Violence*, 14(8): 821–38.

Ward, T, Hudson, S and Marshall, WL (1996) Attachment Style in Sex Offenders: A preliminary study. *Journal of Sex Research*, 33(1): 17–26.

Williams, G, Murphy, J and Houston, J (2010) Personality, in Banyard, P, Davies, MNO, Norman, C and Winder, B (2010) *Essential Psychology: A concise introduction*. London: Sage.

Winter, D (2003) Slot Rattling, in Horley, J (ed.) *Personal Construct Perspectives on Forensic Psychology*. Hove: Brunner-Routledge.

Yates, P (2009) Is Denial Related to Sex Offence Risk and Recidivism? A review and treatment implications. *Psychology, Crime and Law*, 15(2/3): 183–99.

Yochelson, S and Samenow, SE (1976) *The Criminal Personality, volume I: A profile for change*. New York: Jason Aronson.

USEFUL WEBSITES

http://dfp.bps.org.uk – Division of Forensic Psychology, British Psychological Society

http://eapl.eu – European Association of Psychology and Law

http://homeoffice.gov.uk/science-research/research-statistics – Home Office research and statistics on crime and related topics

www.crim.cam.ac.uk – Institute of Criminology, University of Cambridge

www.justice.gov.uk/about/noms – National Offender Management Service

www2.lse.ac.uk/socialPolicy/researchcentresandgroups/mannheim/Home.aspx – Mannheim Centre for Criminology, London School of Economics

3 Policing, attributions, stereotypes and prejudice

C H A P T E R   O B J E C T I V E S

By the end of this chapter you should be able to:

- understand how people form attributions, stereotypes and prejudices;
- appreciate the link between stereotypes, prejudice and discriminations;
- understand and evaluate the implications of these for police officers and for police work;
- apply your learning from the chapter through the case studies provided.

L I N K S   T O   S T A N D A R D S

This chapter provides opportunities for links with the following Skills for Justice, National Occupational Standards (NOS) for Policing and Law Enforcement 2008.

AE1	Maintain and develop your knowledge, skills and competence.
CA1	Use law enforcement actions in a fair and justified way.
SFJAA1	Promote equality and value diversity.
POL1A1	Use police action in a fair and justified way.
BE2	Provide initial support to victims, survivors and witnesses, and assess their need for further support.

With the introduction of the Qualification and Credit Framework (QCF), it is likely that the term 'National Occupational Standards' will change. At the time of writing, it is not clear what the new title will be, although it is known that some organisations will use the term 'QCF assessment units'.

Links to current NOS are provided at the start of each chapter; however, it should be noted that these are currently subject to review and it is recommended that you visit the Skills for Justice website to check the currency of all the NOS provided: www.skillsforjustice-nosfinder.com.

Introduction

The police have come under intense scrutiny in recent times due to some of the decision-making processes in high-profile cases (e.g.see Macpherson, 1999). This has had significant consequences for the police force and on the public's perception of the police. For example, the Scarman (1982) report into the Brixton riots found a disproportionate use of stop and search powers against black people. Then, over a decade later, the Macpherson report (1999) argued that the investigation into the death of Stephen Lawrence was marred by professional incompetence and institutionalised racism. Officers involved in these cases made errors attributable, in part, to racial stereotypes, prejudices and poor decision making. In this chapter we explore psychological theories of how people explain the behaviour of others and their own behaviour, as well as how people form stereotypes and perceptions of others. Understanding these processes is vitally important for police officers as their actions matter, have consequences for others and are often subject to scrutiny. While past cases have highlighted some of the errors in police officers' judgement, it is important to realise that they are errors that all humans make. However, by developing an awareness of these issues, police officers can be better informed about the decisions they make.

Social categorisation and stereotyping

In order to make sense out of things, humans often categorise them as being similar to some objects (e.g. cars can be classed as similar to vans) and different from others (e.g. cars are not the same as pedestrians) (Gregson et al., 2010). This process can take place on an individual level and on a group level. For instance, we can distinguish between members of one group (police officers) and another group (victims). In our everyday lives we often divide people and ourselves into categories that allow us to distinguish between people (Brewer and Crano, 1994). When we categorise someone we tend to react to that person or group in a stereotypical way (Ainsworth, 2002). When behaviour is directed at a person because of their affiliation with a certain group, 'discrimination' occurs. Thus, key concepts within social categorisation are 'stereotypes' and 'prejudice'.

Stereotypes can be defined as beliefs that *mark out certain objects as familiar or strange, emphasising the difference, so that the slightly familiar and the somewhat strange are sharply alien* (Lippman, 1922, p59). Tajfel defines stereotypes as *the attribution of general psychological characteristics to large human groups* (1981, p132). In short, stereotypes are mental short cuts that allow people to save time and effort when processing information about others. The list of stereotypes that can be witnessed in everyday life is seemingly endless; for example, 'accountants are dull', 'used cars salesmen can't be trusted' or 'sportsmen have poor IQs' (Brehm et al., 1999). Although stereotypes may not be inherently bad (they can help make sense of the world – Hamilton and Crump, 2004), they are generalised, oversimplified impressions of someone or something (Gregson et al., 2010). It is because of this that stereotypes can lead to discrimination (see Figure 3.1).

Discrimination can be caused through stereotyping and through prejudice, with a reinforcing relationship between stereotyping and prejudice. There are thus clear links between the three phenomena. For instance, discriminatory practices may support stereotypes and prejudice. Stereotypes may lead someone to become prejudiced, with prejudiced people perhaps using stereotypes to legitimise their world views (Brehm et al., 1999). We will look at these processes in greater detail throughout this chapter.

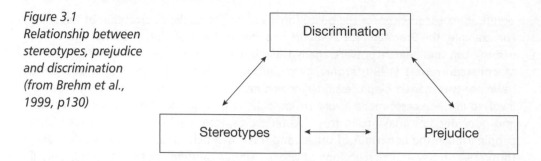

Figure 3.1
Relationship between
stereotypes, prejudice
and discrimination
(from Brehm et al.,
1999, p130)

There are serious dangers when forming stereotypes, which blind us to the individual differences within and between groups. For example, a stereotype may lead you to believe that young Afro-Caribbean men are more likely to be involved with drugs, which may lead to the presumption that *all* young Afro-Caribbean men are involved in drugs (Ainsworth, 2002). This stereotype caused an over-representation of the black population in arrest statistics in the late 1970s and early 1980s. These stereotypes caused discrimination as police officers were using stop and search (e.g. 'sus' law) powers disproportionately against the black population (Carr-Hill and Drew, 1990). It was the disproportionate use of 'sus' laws through operation Swamp 81 that was a key instigator in the Brixton riots in 1981.

REFLECTIVE TASK

- *We all hold stereotypical views about things in our lives. Think about the stereotypes you may form in your daily lives (e.g. 'women can't reverse park', 'men can't discuss their emotions') and make a note of them.*

- *Now think about how these stereotypes could bias your thinking in certain settings and consider what impact stereotypical thinking could have on police work.*

Social identity theory

Social identity theory can be associated with stereotypes and discrimination. Tajfel and Turner (1979) contend that people's self-concepts and self-esteem are not simply derived from individual personal identity and status, but also from the status and achievements of the groups they belong to and are affiliated with (Tajfel and Turner, 1979). The crux of social identity theory is that individuals need to achieve a positive social identity and have a want to be positively evaluated (Taylor and Moghaddam, 1994). Tajfel et al. (1971) conducted a series of experiments to ascertain the minimal conditions in which a person would be biased towards an in-group (e.g. favouring the group to which they belong over another). In their classic experiment, participants were randomly assigned to one of two groups (although participants were told this was based on their preference for paintings by Klee or Kandinsky). The task in the experiment for the participants was to assign points (worth money) to fellow participants in the study. However, participants were told to which group the individuals belonged (e.g. there was a choice of two individuals to share the points between – one was in their group and the other was not). The findings were interesting; participants allocated more points to the participant in their group (despite not knowing them and the groups being arbitrarily assigned). In short, they discriminated in favour of their in-group. The surprising aspect of Tajfel et al.'s (1971) results was the minimal conditions needed for in-group bias to occur; indeed, the mere presence of an in-group gave rise to discrimination.

It has been argued that becoming a police officer is a defining identity, so that being part of the group 'police' becomes engrained in one's social identity. Ahern argues that, when someone becomes a police officer, *[he leaves] society behind to enter a profession that does more than give him a job, it defines who he is. He will always be a cop* (quoted in Skolnick, 2008, p35). The social identity of being 'police officers' will naturally dispose officers to show bias towards that group and protect it from threat. There are positive and negative aspects to such a social identity and these can be seen in the main aspects of cop culture (see, e.g., Reiner, 1997). Two of these aspects are 'internal solidarity' and 'social isolation'. The former comes from confronting shared grave danger, backing each other up and being part of a 'brotherhood' of police officers (Skolnick, 2008). The latter is a product of the organisational framework of police work, for example a shift system and the need to maintain social distance (Reiner, 1997).

It has been argued that police officers are 'emotional labourers' (see, e.g., Winter, 2003), as discussed more fully in Chapter 7, as they constantly have to use their emotions throughout their working life. However, this aspect of cop culture can be problematic and can result in discriminatory practice. The internal solidarity can be used to shield wrongdoing, while social isolation can *exacerbate the unrealistic or prejudiced stereotypes underlying discrimination* (Reiner, 1997, p1017). Thus, the police officer's social identity can serve to protect the interests of the police who violate the law (Skolnick, 2008). It can also lead to negative appraisal, criticism or feedback being dismissed. A recent study by Foster (2008) found that police officers still maintained that the Stephen Lawrence murder was not due to institutional racism and that racism was a peripheral or irrelevant factor in the handling of the case.

REFLECTIVE TASK

Search YouTube for documentary clips about the Brixton riots in 1981, for example www.youtube.com/watch?v=oIN23LFGtw8. Then consider the following.

- *In what ways did stereotypical and prejudice attitudes contribute to the riots?*

- *In what ways could the police have prevented the riots from happening?*

Prejudice

Racism

So far we have noted how humans form stereotypes and how discrimination can occur. This chapter now looks in greater detail at different kinds of prejudice and the challenges these have for a police officer's role. Racial prejudice was first defined by George Allport as:

> *an antipathy based on faulty and inflexible generalisation. It may be felt or expressed. It may be directed towards a [racial] group as a whole, or towards an individual because he is a member of that group.*

(1954, p280)

This quote highlights an important dualism in that racial prejudice can be experienced on both the individual and group level. It is important to note that there are multiple levels of racism. On the individual level, everyone is capable of being racist towards others, yet there are also institutional and cultural factors that privilege some members of society (generally the dominant groups) and discriminate against others (Brehm et al., 1999).

One of the crucial features of contemporary racism is its 'denial', manifested typically in phrases such as 'I have nothing against blacks but . . .' (van Dijk, 1992). The 'denial of racism' has been found to be prevalent in much of police officers' discourse about the Lawrence Inquiry, with many officers unaware of the potential for unwitting discriminatory behaviour in their investigations (Foster, 2008). In some ways this is unsurprising. Various studies have shown that even the most ardent prejudiced person will use social desirability and impression management tactics to present themselves and their group in a positive light and will go to great lengths to avoid and suppress their prejudices (van Dijk, 1992). For instance, in the contemporary political arena, implicit prejudicial views have sought to be legitimised through official governmental parties such as the British Nationalist Party (BNP). This is not to suggest that the police are inherently racist or that they hold views akin to the BNP. Instead, it highlights that, in the police's case, the desire not to be seen as racist can blind officers to the discriminatory (albeit perhaps unintentional) practices in their police work.

Rape myths and sex role stereotyping

It was Martha Burt who first coined the term 'rape myths', which she argued were the *prejudicial, stereotyped, or false beliefs about rape, rape victims and rapists* (1980, p217). Rape myths serve to justify and legitimise rape. Lonsway and Fitzgerald (1994) expanded on the work of Burt (1980) and defined rape myths as *attitudes and beliefs that are generally false but are widely and persistently held, and that serve to deny and justify male sexual aggression against women* (1994, p134). Rape myth acceptance can be seen as a way of justifying and legitimising the rapist's behaviour, while shifting blame on to the victim as she 'deserved it', 'wanted it', 'dressed provocatively' or 'lied' and because 'nice girls don't get raped'.

Rape myth acceptance is a serious problem and has real consequences for the victims of rape and their reporting of the offence. The subscription to rape myths can play a role in victim blaming and facilitate the view that the woman played some part in the rape. Girard and Senn's (2008) study on undergraduate students' (n=280) perceptions of the effect of voluntary and involuntary drug use on attributions about sexual assault found that women were seen as playing a continuing role if they had voluntarily consumed drugs prior to the offence. While participants assigned blame to the perpetrator in sexual assaults facilitated by alcohol or drugs, women's voluntary consumption of drugs prior to a sexual assault increased victim blame (Girard and Senn, 2008).

Worryingly, the same use of rape myths has been found to influence jurors' decision making in cases of rape. Finch and Munro (2005) found that jurors frequently held views about the attribution of blame and responsibility that were inconsistent with the application of the law. Jurors were found to consider many extra-legal factors when reaching a decision. These included rape myths and stereotypical conceptions about intoxication, sexual assault and drug-facilitated rape. Finch and Munro (2005) also found a surprising level of condemnation for victims, with victims generally blamed unless there was clear evidence that the perpetrator had committed wrongdoing. This has been demonstrated further by the reduction in compensation for those victims of rape who had consumed alcohol at the time of the offence, as it was judged to be a contributing factor to the offence (Williams, 2008). Furthermore, it has been found that the police sometimes dismiss claims of rape if the victim is seen to be partly to blame or if they had 'instigated' the offence (Buddie and Miller, 2001).

CASE STUDY

An attractive young woman wearing a revealing, low-cut top and short skirt approaches the bar. A man offers to buy her a drink; she agrees and, on receiving the drink, she flirtatiously smiles and winks and then leaves the man. She goes to the toilets and the man follows. She later reports to security at the bar that she has been raped.

(Adapted from Pemberton, 2011)

In this case study is a pictorial of the rape myth that a woman raped while wearing revealing clothing is to blame, as she is inviting the offence and leading the man on. This poster formed part of a campaign by Rape Crisis Scotland to confront these widely held beliefs and attitudes. Societal attitudes, then, continue to play a significant role in limiting justice for women who have experienced rape.

- *Consider the picture in the case study above and visit the Fawcett Society for some widely held myths and facts about rape: www.fawcettsociety.org.uk/index.asp?Page ID=593.*

- *How might 'rape myth acceptance' by a police officer affect the victim in this case? What issues would police officers have to be mindful of in this case?*

Attributions

When someone does something, we usually attribute a cause to their behaviour. Similarly, when we do something we attribute a cause in order to explain it. This section considers the decisions we make when deciding why things have happened (Meredith and Witty, 2010). It has been argued that people make sense of other people's behaviour as 'naive scientists' – we seek to understand the behaviour in others in a stable and rational way (Heider, 1958).

CASE STUDIES

Case study 1

An elderly woman is walking down a road late one evening on her way home from the supermarket when a man shouts something at her. She stops and the man runs towards her, attacks her and steals her purse. The elderly woman is left with cuts and grazes to her face and is deeply affected by the incident.

Case study 2

An aggressive-looking skinhead with tattoos is walking down a road late one evening, after having a few drinks at his local pub, when a man shouts something at him and then starts to attack him. The skinhead is left with cuts and grazes to his face and is deeply affected by the incident.

REFLECTIVE TASK

- *Think about the characteristics of the victims in the two case studies above. Now describe each victim in three words (and be honest . . .).*

- *Who elicits the most sympathy? What implications could this have for support and advice for the victim?*

Internal and external attributions

Attributions can be internal or external.

- Internal attributions focus on internal or dispositional states.

- External attributions seek to explain the behaviour of the individual or the event in terms of the situation or the environment.

For example, if you do not perform well in your end-of-year exams you could tell yourself or your parents that 'I'm not clever enough', that is, you make an internal attribution. Or you could say 'I didn't do well because I drank too much the night before, I didn't revise and I was late for the exam', that is, you make an external or situational attribution. Attributions can also be stable or unstable, controllable or uncontrollable. A stable attribution is one that may reflect consistent behaviour within an individual, whereas an unstable attribution will reflect a one-off 'out of character' act. For instance, someone who kills or injures another person in self-defence will be judged less harshly than someone who kills another, but is motivated to do so and has a long history of grievous bodily harm (GBH). In the former, the behaviour of the person is unstable and not likely to be repeated; however, in the latter it appears to be a stable factor in their offending. The controllability/uncontrollability dimension relates to how much control the person is perceived to have over their behaviour. For example, a female officer who arrests large numbers of men for kerb crawling may be doing so not because she has a desire to see men who use prostitutes punished, but because she has been commanded to do so by her senior officer (Ainsworth, 2002).

The way we make attributions about people can be biased, inaccurate or false and so, as those interested in policing and police work, it is important that we have an awareness of how attributions are made or shaped and the effect they can have on perceptions. Jones and Nisbett (1972) found that humans have a tendency to explain their own behaviour in terms of situational factors, whereas we are more likely to assume personal/internal dispositions about the behaviour of others. How often during the run-up to elections have we heard politicians promise a crackdown on individuals committing anti-social behaviour? Such people are generally discussed in dispositional terms – 'bad lads' or 'morally corrupt'. However, when something goes wrong within their party or their leadership is called into question, politicians are more likely to make situational attributions. For instance, the economy is bad because of the global recession and previous political party mistakes; it is not due to poor national and local policy or leadership. Using the example of a hooded individual causing anti-social behaviour, are we more likely to explain his behaviour in terms of internal disposition or situational attribution? If we are honest, it is most likely going to be the former. We are more likely to think that they are bad, rather than reacting to their environment or situation, for example social exclusion, isolation and are living (most probably) in socially disadvantaged areas.

The real question, then, is do attributions actually matter both generally and for policing? Well, according to research, both in terms of criminality and general psychological well-being, the answer may well be yes. Indeed, when accounting for negative events, research has shown that shifting casual attributions away from internal stable dispositions (e.g. 'I failed because I'm stupid') to external, unstable ones can maintain psychological well-being and has been linked to crime desistance (i.e. persistent criminals stopping their criminal activity) (Maruna, 2004). Linked to this, Martin Seligman's (1975) learned help-lessness theory proposed that depressed people had learned to view themselves as unable to cope with and control events. In essence, they made a stable attribution – 'nothing I can do can change anything' – and this developed into negative responses such as helplessness and passivity.

Maruna (2001, 2004) has applied attributional theory to those desisting from criminality. He found that crime desisters were more likely to see their criminal selves as qualitatively different from themselves now. Maruna (2001) argued that crime desisters had supplied themselves with 'redemption scripts', which meant they viewed themselves as 'good people who had done bad things'. Rather than being bad people who were doomed to a life of deviance, 'crime desisters' viewed their offending as external and unstable. Crime persisters, on the other hand, viewed themselves as 'bad people who do bad things' (they subscribed to 'condemnation scripts') and they saw their offending as part of them (e.g. part of their history, who they are now and in the future), and so it was internal and stable.

However, when we interact with criminal populations we may, to some degree, affect their behaviour. If we react to young people as troublemakers, and if we label them and respond to them harshly, they may conform to that label and act accordingly. This process has been termed 'secondary deviation' and occurs when individuals assimilate such labels into their social identity (Lemert, 1951).

Related to the last point are the concepts of 'labelling' and the 'self-fulfilling prophecy'. The self-fulfilling prophecy suggests that an expectation of something can actually lead to its own fulfilment. This concept suggests that other people's perceptions shape who we are and there is a considerable body of work that supports the assertion that people come to acquire identities that are attributed to them by others (Burr, 2002). According to Becker (1963), criminals are not criminals until they successfully acquire that label. If the label becomes internalised, they are more likely to act and respond to people according to that label. Thus, labels are conferred on people by people, and once labelled the label becomes a part of that person's identity. Just as we may label a jar 'coffee' because of what is inside the jar (and what we expect to be in it), we have expectations and beliefs about the people we label (Burr, 2002).

Fundamental attribution error

The fundamental attribution error is the tendency of humans to overestimate a person's dispositional/internal state and underemphasise the external situation (the environment/ context) (Ross, 1977). When we perceive other people we have a strong inclination to overestimate dispositional factors and ignore other factors. This is particularly the case when we make inferences about a person from a single event. We attribute the perception of a person's behaviour in a particular event as being stable and enduring; that is, it is consistent with their daily behaviour (Brewer and Crano, 1994).

Imagine you are walking in town minding your own business when a man in a rush bumps into you and rushes off without offering an apology. It would not be uncommon for us to say 'what a rude man' and make the generalisation that he is a rude person. This is the fundamental attribution error; we have overestimated the dispositional state of the man's behaviour – we believe his behaviour was due to his being rude. However, it may just as well have been a situational or environmental factor that contributed to his behaviour. The man may have been in a hurry because of some emergency or crisis and so may not have been thinking straight. In most other circumstances, he could be the most pleasant man you would want to meet. Think about this in terms of lecturers and teachers: how many of you would think they are uptight, authoritarian, harsh or boring, etc? However, you may be shocked and surprised to see their behaviour with family and friends, at parties or at other social events. A more serious problem is when we consider cases of sexual abuse. For instance, child offenders are skilled at convincing families that they are decent, respectable people and because of this they are able to gain trust of parents and overcome barriers that may restrict access to children (Finkelhor, 1984). Indeed, the stereotypical image of a sexual offender as being a dirty old man with thick glasses is dangerous and misguided, and blinds us to the fact that sexual offenders are from all walks of life and from all social areas and that often such people lead 'double lives' (Salter, 2001).

The problem such errors cause here is that they can lead to victim blaming and dis-believing; people do not want to think that their doctor, neighbour or local police officer is capable of an offence and would rather give people the benefit of the doubt because of their respected status. This form of error is the belief that a person in a respected position always acts respectfully. As noted earlier concerning the issue of rape myths, such stereo-typical views can be dangerous. Goodey (2005) has found that the fear of being asked uncomfortable questions is one of the main reasons for the high attrition rates in rape cases. For instance, in 2002, 11,678 rape offences reached court out of an estimated 50,000 incidences of rape. There were, however, only 655 convictions, 258 of which were due to a guilty plea, which means that, in all the cases for that year, only 3.4 per cent were believed (Kelly et al., 2005). Possible explanations for this could be prejudicial rape myths, errors in attribution by jurors, poor decision making by the police or widely held societal beliefs.

Fundamental attribution and criminal justice

We can apply the concept of fundamental attribution error to many aspects of the criminal justice system (CJS). Criminal law would assert that criminal behaviour is the free choice of individuals, when in actuality human behavioural responses vary much less across situations than is commonly thought (Dripps, 2003). For instance, it has been argued that crime is much more of a problem for and in socially deprived and dis-advantaged communities (Lea and Young, 1984). Crime in those communities is likely to be due to situation, for example not having access to resources or opportunities, living in environments where criminality is accepted, or relative deprivation, rather than it being due to the individuals in those communities being inherently criminogenic. However, the CJS calls for its workers to evaluate the personal responsibility of criminals and this process affects punishment (e.g. if you are taking responsibility for your actions by pleading guilty you may get a shorter sentence). Criminal justice professionals, whether they are police officers, judges, solicitors, court workers or jurors, are thus predisposed towards attri-buting conduct and its consequences to personality (Dripps, 2003). A further example in policing may be witnessing a driver speeding. You may perceive the driver as someone who is reckless, who disregards the law and who does not care about the lives of others. You may pursue the driver and, upon pulling him or her over, adopt an authoritarian and stern interpersonal style. However, the person may be distraught and visibly crying, telling you that his or her son has been taken ill and is fighting for his life in hospital. It is clear that, in this case, the behaviour is being driven by the external factor.

The fundamental attribution error can also be used in the applied criminal justice setting of offender behaviour therapy. In such settings excuse making and assigning blame externally, for example 'it wasn't my fault', is seen as maladaptive and is often given the label 'cognitive distortion'. Maruna and Mann (2006) are critical of the assumption that, after the event, excuses are inherently 'bad' or criminogenic. They argue that clinicians and academics have been guilty of something akin to the fundamental attribution error. They suggest that criminal justice professionals are too focused on having offenders 'take responsibility', which may, in fact, be counterproductive (Maruna and Mann, 2006). Generally, when people account for their actions (particularly a transgression or something that is considered 'wrong'), it is normal for them to assign blame elsewhere or to explain their behaviour in terms of external circumstances (Dean et al., 2007). Indeed, as mentioned earlier, when accounting for negative events, research has shown that shifting casual attributions away from internal stable dispositions to external unstable ones can maintain psychological well-being and, as noted, has been linked to crime desistance (Snyder and Higgins, 1988; Maruna, 2004).

REFLECTIVE TASK

Think about the aggressive-looking skinhead from the previous case study on page 30.

- *How might police make the fundamental attribution error with him?*

- *How might this affect support and advice from the police and his experience with the CJS?*

- *In the last reflective task on page 30, you were asked to describe the victim in three words. What were those three words? Did they differ between victims?*

In terms of the tattooed male victim, we may make the fundamental attribution error when dealing with him if we make a dispositional attribution for his behaviour. We may decide that he is the architect of his own downfall and that probably he deserved it because he must have provoked the incident. He looks aggressive, therefore he must be, and so cannot be blameless for the incident. We are more likely to ascribe external causes to the second victim, who was seen as vulnerable and frail, blameless and thus not at fault. Notice here how our perceptions and attributions can be guided by enduring stereotypes.

Making an impression

So far this chapter has focused on how we perceive individuals and groups, and what this can mean for policing and the CJS. We now look at how people form perceptions about us and how we initially form perceptions of others. There is an old cliché, 'you only get one chance to make a good first impression', and this is especially relevant to policing. Studies have found that victims form perceptions about police officers from every aspect of an officer's behaviour (Stephens and Sinden, 2000). The police officer's initial response is likely to shape the victim's experience of the CJS. Indeed, the police's initial response to the victim is their 'first contact' with a criminal justice agency, so it is important that police officers make a good first impression. Now, more than ever, the police service is concerned with its public image and chiefly with public (sometimes termed 'customer') satisfaction. The introduction of the now abandoned 'Policing Pledge' shifted rhetoric from performance targets to customer satisfaction, which now means that the public are centre stage in determining police performance (Fleming and McLaughlin, 2010; O'Connor, 2010). Indeed, part of the challenge of modern policing is engaging positively with the community and earning their confidence and trust. The issue of public confidence has thus become an important policy issue within policing (Fleming and McLaughlin, 2010).

When we initially form a perception of someone it is generally based on a few select areas: facial appearance, hairstyle and clothing, physique and voice (including pitch). In terms of policing, how often have we heard the phrases 'his face doesn't fit' or 'I don't like the look of him' (Ainsworth, 2002). So what can help police officers make a good impression with victims of crime? Stephens and Sinden (2000) found that officers who were attentive and listened, for example were not just concerned with getting the facts, and who showed understanding and concern, were perceived positively by victims. This may have been due to 'facial appearance', looking interested and concerned, their body language (physique) and perhaps how they spoke to the victims, for example in a reassuring and empathetic tone (voice and pitch). In the same research it was found that a no-nonsense style of policing, where the victims are seen as witnesses to extract information from, was perceived as rude and lacking compassion (Stephens and Sinden, 2000). Such officers may have looked uninterested, in a rush or not bothered about the plight of the victims. They may have had closed body language and spoken in a more abrupt tone. We shall explore the importance of interpersonal and communication skills in Chapter 4.

We tend to form an impression of a person quickly on a few select criteria and then generalise that impression to traits of that person. This process is similar to the fundamental attribution error discussed earlier. Forming perceptions of people can be seen as 'inferential' because we observe the appearance and behaviour of people and from that infer things about them. When working with victims of crime, it is important that they have a positive experience of the police and this is now a central aspect of modern policing. While the Policing Pledge is now redundant, many force areas still uphold the tenets of the pledge or still use it as the benchmark for their service delivery to the public. For example, the Metropolitan Police Service's pledge, 'Our Promise to the Public', states that public satisfaction with the police can be seen as a barometer for public confidence. The pledge outlines that the police will always treat the public fairly, with dignity and respect, ensuring that everyone has access to the service at a time that is reasonable and suitable (www.met.police.uk). By forming a good impression, police officers can also help guard against secondary victimisation, which results from the insensitive treatment of victims of crime – often inadvertently – by the CJS (Goodey, 2005). For instance, if victims are interviewed in a way that appears to question the veracity of their version of events, so casting doubt on the truthfulness of their accounts, victims may become re-victimised through their dealings with the CJS (see Chapter 4 on interpersonal skills, which covers this issue in much greater detail).

However, our perception of things is not always a clear-cut or straightforward process. Look at the images in Figures 3.2 and 3.3 and note what you see.

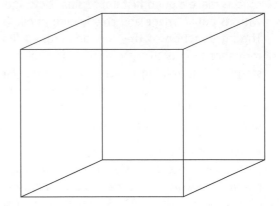

Figure 3.2   *Figure 3.3*

Figure 3.2 can be perceived as either two faces or a single vase, while the other image, known as the Necker cube, represents a three-dimensional object positioned in two-dimensional space. If you stare at it long enough the cube changes its orientation. If we do not look closely enough our brain interprets one image and maintains it. It is only when looking closely that our perspective changes. This process is the same for many of the social psychological concepts discussed in this chapter. How we form stereotypes, our prejudices and how these affect our interactions are only considered once we reflect on them. We can do this through reflecting on our experiences, and police officers can do this by reflecting on their interactions with a potential criminal or a victim. There is a book in this series that focuses on reflection in police officers and it is recommended that you read this (see Copley, 2011).

C H A P T E R   S U M M A R Y

This chapter has focused on how we form stereotypes, attributions and perceptions of others, assessed the consequences these can have for discrimination and prejudice, and evaluated the impact these can have on the role of the police officer. Stereotyping, making errors in attribution and forming perceptions based on limited information (e.g. first impressions) is something we all do as humans; however, the issue is magnified for police officers as their biased decision making can have real consequences for individuals and society. An increased awareness of human attribution and perception formation ensures we can be more mindful of our actions and are clear about the possible consequences of our behaviour.

FURTHER READING

Burt, MR (1980) Cultural Myths and Supports for Rape. *Journal of Personality and Social Psychology*, 38(2): 217–30.

Dripps, DA (2003) Fundamental Retribution Error: Criminal justice and the social psychology of blame. *Vanderbilt Law Review*, 56(5): 1381–438.

Finch, E and Munro, VE (2005) Juror Stereotypes in Blame Attribution in Rape Cases Involving Intoxicants. *British Journal of Criminology*, 45: 25–38.

Tajfel, H, Billig, MG, Bundy, RP and Flament, C (1971) Social Categorization and Intergroup Behaviour. *European Journal of Social Psychology*, 1: 149–77.

REFERENCES

Ainsworth, PB (2002) *Psychology and Policing*. Cullompton: Willan.

Allport, GW (1954) *The Nature of Prejudice*. Cambridge, MA: Addison-Wesley.

Becker, HS (1963) *Outsiders.* London: Collier-Macmillan.

Brehm, SS, Kassin, SM and Fein, S (1999) *Social Psychology.* New York: Houghton Mifflin.

Brewer, MB and Crano, WD (1994) *Social Psychology.* New York: West.

Buddie, AM and Miller, AG (2001) Beyond Rape Myths: A more complex view of perceptions of rape victims, 45(3–4): 139–60.

Burr, V (2002) *The Person in Social Psychology.* Hove: Psychology Press.

Burt, MR (1980) Cultural Myths and Supports for Rape. *Journal of Personality and Social Psychology*, 38(2): 217–30.

Carr-Hill, R and Drew, D (1990) Blacks, Police and Crime, in Bhat, A, Carr-Hill, R and Ohri, S (eds) *Britain's Black Population: A new perspective.* Aldershot: Gower.

Copley, S (2011) *Reflective Practice for Policing Students.* Exeter: Learning Matters.

Dean, C, Mann, RE, Milner, R and Maruna, S (2007) Changing Child Sex Abusers' Cognition, in Gannon, TA, Ward, T, Beech, AR and Fisher, D (eds) *Aggressive Offenders' Cognition: Theory, research and practice.* Chichester: John Wiley.

Dripps, DA (2003) Fundamental Retribution Error: Criminal justice and the social psychology of blame. *Vanderbilt Law Review*, 56(5): 1381–438.

Finch, E and Munro, VE (2005) Juror Stereotypes in Blame Attribution in Rape Cases Involving Intoxicants. *British Journal of Criminology*, 45: 25–38.

Finkelhor, D (1984) *Child Sexual Abuse: New theory and research.* New York: The Free Press.

Fleming, J and McLaughlin, E (2010) 'The Public Gets what the Public Wants?' Interrogating the 'public confidence' agenda. *Policing*, 4(3): 199–202.

Foster, J (2008) 'It Might Have Been Incompetent, but it Wasn't Racist': Murder detectives' perceptions of the Lawrence inquiry and its impact on homicide investigation in London. *Policing and Society*, 18(2): 89–112.

Girard, AL and Senn, CY (2008) The Role of New 'Date Rape Drugs' in Attributions about Date Rape. *Journal of Interpersonal Violence*, 23(1): 3–20.

Goodey, J (2005) *Victims and Victimology: Research, policy and practice.* Harrow: Pearson Longman.

Gregson, M, Hill, R and Blagden, N (2010) Behaviour Between Groups, in Banyard, P, Davies, MNO, Norman, C and Winder, B (eds) *Essential Psychology: A concise introduction.* London: Sage.

Hamilton, DL and Crump, SA (2004) Stereotypes, in Spielberger, C (ed.) *Encyclopaedia of Applied Psychology.* New York: Elsevier.

Heider, F (1958) *The Psychology of Interpersonal Relations.* Chichester: John Wiley.

Jones, EE and Nisbett, RE (1972) The Actor and the Observer: Divergent perceptions of the causes of behavior, in Jones, EE, Kanouse, DE, Kelley, HH, Nisbett, RE, Valins, S and Weiner, B (eds) *Attribution: Perceiving the causes of behavior*. Morristown, NJ: General Learning Press.

Kelly, L, Lovett, J and Regan, L (2005) *Gap or Chasm? Attrition in reported rape cases.* London: Home Office.

Lemert, EM (1951) *Social Pathology*. New York: McGraw-Hill.

Lea, J and Young, J (1984) *What Is to Be Done about Law and Order?* London: Pluto Press.

Lippmann, W (1922) *Public Opinion.* London: Allen & Unwin.

Lonsway, KA and Fitzgerald, LF (1994) Rape Myths: In review. *Psychology of Women Quarterly*, 18: 133–64.

Macpherson, Sir William (1999) *Report of the Stephen Lawrence Inquiry.* London: HMSO.

Maruna, S (2001) *Making Good: How ex-convicts reform and rebuild their lives.* Washington, DC: American Psychological Association.

Maruna, S (2004) Desistance and Explanatory Style: A new direction in the psychology of reform. *Journal of Contemporary Criminal Justice*, 20: 184–200.

Maruna, S and Mann, R (2006) A Fundamental Attribution Error? Rethinking cognitive distortions. *Legal and Criminological Psychology*, 11(2): 155–77.

Meredith, A and Whitty, M (2010) Social Judgments and Behaviour, in Banyard, P, Davies, MNO, Norman, C and Winder, B (2010) *Essential Psychology: A concise introduction.* London: Sage.

O'Connor, D (2010) Performance From the Outside-In. *Policing*, 4(2): 152–6.

Pemberton, S (2011) Unpublished PhD thesis, Nottingham Trent University.

Reiner, R (1997) Policing and the Media, in Newburn, T (ed.) *Handbook of Policing.* Cullompton: Willan.

Ross, L (1977) The Intuitive Psychologist and his Shortcomings: Distortions in the attribution process, in Berkowitz, L (ed.) *Advances in Experimental Social Psychology*, vol. 10. New York: Academic.

Salter, AC (2001) *Predators: Pedophiles, rapists and other sex offenders.* New York: Basic Books.

Scarman, L (1982) *The Scarman Report: The Brixton disorders, 10–12 April 1981: Report of an inquiry.* Harmondsworth: Penguin.

Seligman, MEP (1975) *Helplessness: On depression, development & death.* San Francisco, CA: Freeman.

Skolnick, J (2008) Enduring Issues of Police Culture and Demographics. *Policing and Society*, 18(1): 34–45.

Snyder, CR and Higgins, RL (1988) Excuses: Their effective role in the negotiation of reality. *Psychological Bulletin*, 104(1): 23–35.

Stephens, B and Sinden, P (2000) Victims' Voices: Domestic assault victims' perceptions of police demeanor. *Journal of Interpersonal Violence*, 15: 534–47.

Tajfel, H (1981) *Human Groups and Social Categories: Studies in social psychology.* Cambridge: Cambridge University Press.

Tajfel, H and Turner, JC (1979). An Integrative Theory of Intergroup Conflict, in Austin, WG and Worchel, S (eds) *The Social Psychology of Intergroup Relations.* Monterey, CA: Brooks/Cole.

Tajfel, H, Billig, MG, Bundy, RP and Flament, C (1971) Social Categorization and Intergroup Behaviour. *European Journal of Social Psychology*, 1: 149–77.

Taylor, DM and Moghaddam, FM (1994) *Theories of Intergroup Relations: International social psychological perspectives.* Westport, CT: Greenwood.

van Dijk, TA (1992) Discourse and the Denial of Racism. *Discourse and Society*, 3: 87–118.

Williams, R (2008) I Did My Bit in Reporting a Rapist, the Authorities Didn't Do Theirs. *The Guardian*, 16 August. Online at www.guardian.co.uk/uk/2008/aug/16/rape.police (accessed 1 February 2010).

Winter, D (2003) Stress in Police Officers: A personal construct theory perspective, in Horley, J (ed.) *Personal Construct Perspectives on Forensic Psychology.* Hove: Brunner-Routledge.

USEFUL WEBSITES

www.hmic.gov.uk/Pages/home.aspx – Her Majesty's Inspectorate of Constabulary

www.homeoffice.gov.uk/police – Home Office information on the police

www.met.police.uk/about/performance/confidence.htm – Metropolitan Police, Public Attitude Survey

4 Communication, interpersonal and interviewing skills

CHAPTER OBJECTIVES

By the end of this chapter you should be able to:

- understand the key interviewing and interpersonal skills needed for interactions with potential offenders;
- describe the key interviewing and interpersonal skills needed for interactions with victims;
- apply good interviewing and interpersonal techniques to your professional practice;
- outline the main interviewing techniques used in police settings.

LINKS TO STANDARDS

This chapter provides opportunities for links with the following Skills for Justice, National Occupational Standards (NOS) for Policing and Law Enforcement 2008.

AE1	Maintain and develop your knowledge, skills and competence.
AA1	Promote equality and value diversity.
AB1	Communicate effectively with people.
HA2	Manage your own resources and professional development.
BE2	Provide initial support to victims, survivors and witnesses, and assess their need for further support.
POL1B10	Support individuals with difficult or potentially difficult relationships.
POL2H1	Interview victims and witnesses.

With the introduction of the Qualification and Credit Framework (QCF), it is likely that the term 'National Occupational Standards' will change. At the time of writing, it is not clear what the new title will be, although it is known that some organisations will use the term 'QCF assessment units'.

Links to current NOS are provided at the start of each chapter; however, it should be noted that these are currently subject to review and it is recommended that you visit the Skills for Justice website to check the currency of all the NOS provided: www.skillsforjustice-nosfinder.com.

Introduction

This chapter outlines some of the key skills and concepts that are needed for interviewing both suspects and victims, and reflects on the interpersonal and communication skills necessary for effective policing practice. As a police officer you will need effective interpersonal skills in your daily role, as you are likely to spend large amounts of time dealing with members of the public, often with great variation between one interaction and the next. Thus, police officers need dynamic interpersonal and communication skills, and the ability to tailor their responses to individuals. A person who is a victim of a serious domestic assault, thus making them vulnerable, will need a different approach from a suspect who is being hostile towards the police. Bakker and Heuven (2006) have argued that policing is a profession in which officers can be classed as 'emotional labourers', as they need to engage with their emotions on a daily basis and in varied settings in order to get the job done. Winter (2003) argues that the 'emotionality' of police work can be implicated in the stress that police officers suffer (we examine this is more detail in Chapter 7).

Psychological concepts, theories and research are hugely beneficial for increasing and bolstering police officers' interviewing and interpersonal skills. This chapter considers the interpersonal skills necessary for interacting with victims and suspects. It also outlines the investigative and cognitive interviews, as well as looking at whether it is possible to detect deception. The chapter further draws on psychotherapeutic literature and contends that core concepts from that literature can enhance effective police work with victims of crime.

PRACTICAL TASK

Get a piece of paper and divide it into two columns. In one column write 'what the police want from the victim' and in the other write 'what the victim wants from the police'. Write down what you think both parties want from each other and then reflect on who has the power in the relationship between police and victim.

Interviewing suspects

This chapter is essentially split into two main sections: interviewing suspects and interviewing victims. The chapter then considers the interviewing procedures and interpersonal and communication skills needed for effective interactions with suspects and victims.

Investigative interviewing

The term 'investigative interviewing' was introduced in England and Wales in the 1990s and represented a move away from the police interviewing philosophy of extracting a confession, towards a general evidence-gathering procedure (Gudjonsson, 2007). It was found around this time that police interviewers and interviewing were poor and there were worries that police practice was resulting in an increase in false confessions. As will become apparent in this chapter, there are key differences between the interviewing of 'victims/witnesses' and 'suspects'. The former can be interviewed in their home and their interviews are relatively free from confrontation and accusation (although this is not always the case; some victims of crime, for example rape and domestic violence, may become the 'victims' of victim blaming, for example in what way did their actions contribute to the offence?). The role of the victim in a police interview is about recalling the events and about providing evidence. Suspects, however, are more likely to face an interrogation, which is a more confrontational procedure and involves accusation and persuasion. Suspects, due to being implicated in the offence, are asked about their actions and intentions (Gudjonsson, 2007).

There have been numerous police interview manuals written over the years, although the crux of their philosophy is:

> *most criminal suspects are reluctant to confess because of the shame associated with what they have done and for the legal consequences. In their view a certain amount of pressure, deception, persuasion and manipulation is essential if the truth is to be revealed.*
> (Gudjonsson, 2003, p7)

Interviewing styles in line with this quotation are associated with the 'Reid technique', which relies heavily on manipulating suspects and is also the most widely used interview technique in the USA. The inherent problem with such techniques is that they assume guilt, at times wrongly, and this results in a form of 'tunnel vision', which leads to a pressuring of suspects to confess (Gudjonsson, 2003, 2007).

In an attempt to improve the interviewing skills of police officers (which were seen at the time as too confrontational and as suffering from poor planning), a national training package was developed and rolled out in 1993 (see Home Office circulars 22/1992 and 7/1993). The package introduced the PEACE model of interviewing and was a shift from an accusatory style of interviewing to one based on truth searching, impartiality and information gathering (Walsh and Milne, 2008). There was also an emphasis on using more open-ended questions rather than closed questions, which followed the shift in approach to evidence gathering.

The PEACE model can be broken down as follows.

- **P – Preparation and planning** – This includes gathering knowledge of the case, arranging the interview and ensuring attendance, also making sure the facilities are suitable.

- **E – Engage and explain** – This is the opening phase of the interview where the introductions formally take place, and legal procedures are met and explained (e.g. reading rights and explanation of what the interview will cover).

- **A – Account** – Interviewees are asked to provide their account of events, which will require clarification and challenge at certain points.

- **C – Closure** – Here the interviewer summarises the main points of the interview and provides the suspect with an opportunity to add or change anything.

- **E – Evaluate** – The account and evidence obtained during questioning need to be evaluated (in light of evidence).

(Adapted from Gudjonsson, 2007, pp470–1)

The PEACE model is still the accepted framework for interviewing suspects for police officers. It has been found that training in PEACE can improve interviewing skills, although new police officers feel that more training is required in interviewing techniques (Dando et al., 2008).

Detecting deception

PRACTICAL TASK

How do you know if someone is lying to you? Write down a list of things that shows that a person is lying to you. Revisit this after reading this section. Have your perceptions on lie detection changed?

Being able to detect deception and to recognise the cues of when someone is lying or telling the truth would be hugely beneficial for police officers (and indeed everyone in society). If we could always recognise a lie from a truth, social interaction may be very different. So how do we know when people are lying to us? Research studies about the behavioural cues of lying have reported that people think that liars are more likely to avert their gaze (not look in your eyes), move their hands and feet, fidget and gesture (Bull et al., 2006). The reason why people think like this is due to these cues being useful indicators of nervousness (with liars believed to be more nervous), or because the person is the focus of attention and is therefore likely to avert their gaze and move more. However, the problem is that telling the truth may have the same effect. For instance, innocent suspects may become emotional and have to think hard when questioned by the police, particularly if they perceive the interview as coercive or aggressive. Furthermore, when someone is emotional it is harder to retrieve information and it becomes harder for the person to remember (Bull et al., 2006). So how good are people at detecting deception in others? Well, psychological research consistently finds that we are poor at detecting lying in others and recent research suggests that most people are no better than chance at detecting lying in others (Bull et al., 2006).

So, the general public are not great at detecting deception, but what about police officers – are they better? Again, research suggests that they also have problems in identifying who is lying and who is telling the truth. Research suggests that those who are innocent when in a police interview may give off the same behavioural cues as those who are lying. As has been highlighted in Chapter 3, police officers can make errors in judgement (as we all do) owing to the processes of perception formation and stereotyping. This is further complicated by the motivations and experiences of the offender, who will be used to lying and, in some circumstances, used to leading multiple lives in order to access their victim(s) (see, e.g., Salter, 2001). Vrij suggests that *experienced criminals . . . for whom it is important to make a good impression on others . . . are unlikely to show nervous behaviour when lying* (2000, p51).

A major limitation of some deception studies is that they are not reflective of real-life situations, which tend to be high risk and high stakes (e.g. because the offender has something to lose – such as the loss of their freedom, etc.). For instance, Vrij and Mann (2001) have found that police officers are better at detecting liars from real interviews from offenders than from lab-based examples. However, they also found that those who believed in stereotypical views of deception and deceptive behaviour (e.g. liars fidget) perform less well as lie detectors. It has been found that cues associated with lying are not what we immediately expect. For instance, decreases in blinking and hand/arm movements and an increase in speech pauses are found more in liars than truth tellers (Bull et al., 2006). Vrij contends that this could be due to the increase in 'cognitive load' (i.e. because someone is thinking so hard about their story, there are fewer movements). Interestingly, Vrij et al. (2008) found that getting suspects to recall their stories in reverse order (from ending up at the police station and working backwards) increased 'cognitive load' and that, as a result, it was easier to identify deceivers.

So far we have looked at the behavioural cues, but many researchers (e.g. Vrij and Mann, 2001) found that cues are more identifiable in narratives (people's stories) and speech. As discussed, Vrij et al. (2008) and Vrij and Mann (2001) have put forward the argument that lying, especially in high-stakes situations (e.g. where there is perhaps some perceived risk of being caught), increases cognitive load; that is, the offender has to think hard about their lie. As a result, Vrij and Mann (2001) found that lying utterances (aspects of speech) contained more speech disturbances, longer pauses and slower speech. In a study by McCormack et al. (2009), they asked participants to give two accounts – one of a true autobiographical event and the other of a fabricated event. They found that accounts of fabricated events were limited in contextual details and interactions (e.g. I met X and then . . .) and contained spontaneous justifications. In short, they were more likely to be bare bones accounts (McCormack et al., 2009). This phenomenon has been noted in sexual offenders who are denying their offence. Offenders 'in denial' have been found to give lots of contextual detail, rationalisations and justifications regarding events not related or associated to the offence or time of the offence, but when asked why they were accused, arrested and later convicted, participants would give minimal detail and very few elaborations (Blagden, 2011).

Therapeutic techniques

There are skills within psychotherapeutic literature that could have a significant benefit for the police interviewer. Psychotherapy, particularly cognitive-behavioural therapy, utilises techniques that allow people to talk and disclose information without having to challenge directly their position or make them feel as though they are in an adversarial situation. A clear example of this is in sexual offender treatment programmes (SOTPs). SOTPs aim to address and challenge offence-supportive cognitions and develop new attitudes designed to change pro-offending behaviour (Hollin and Palmer, 2006). In order to do this emphasis is placed on disclosure and offence accounts – in short, the bits offenders do not want to talk about. Thus, therapists have to find constructive ways of engaging the offenders and facilitate the process of them discussing their offence. This section will highlight some of the ways this could be achieved and how they could benefit policing practice.

Motivational interviewing

Motivational interviewing (MI) has developed into a popular technique for encouraging offenders into treatment and helping resolve ambivalence (an offender's mixed feelings) towards aspects of their offending behaviour. MI seeks not *to persuade directly, [instead] the counselor systematically elicits from the client and reinforces reasons for concern and for change, while maintaining a warm and supportive atmosphere for exploration of ambivalent feelings* (Miller, 1996, pp839–40). MI, unlike some investigative interviewing techniques, is critical of the 'confrontation' paradigm of working with clients, which emphasises that denial and deception need challenge and confrontation (Miller and Rollnick, 2002).

MI assumes that people do not disclose information because they have mixed feelings about doing so; for example, they want to tell the truth but are afraid of the consequences (e.g. legal ramifications and shame) and so are motivated to maintain their position. It has been suggested that using MI strategies, such as de-emphasising labels (this may include making people feel safe), de-emphasising negative aspects (e.g. punishment), using reflection of self-motivational statements (in order to reinforce the 'theme'), emphasising personal choice and acknowledging the difficulty in admitting, may aid in decreasing self-protective strategies (see, e.g., Mann and Rollnick, 1996). Confrontation only serves to increase resistance in people. It is not suggested here that such a measure is directly relevant for policing. Such techniques are usually administered during weeks and months, whereas police officers do not have that time. What is being suggested here is that the tenets of motivational interviewing and an understanding of motivation can be beneficial and can add to the police officer's interviewing toolkit.

Although not strictly a motivational approach, Betari's box is a useful interpersonal skill for police officers in many settings. Betari's box, sometimes referred to as the conflict cycle, is a simple model that demonstrates the relationship between attitudes and behaviour and, specifically, how the attitudes and behaviours of one person could influence the attitudes and behaviours of others (Clements and Jones, 2002). The model can be seen in Figure 4.1.

This model is especially relevant for police officers, as you will often be in circumstances of hostility (e.g. town centres on Friday and Saturday nights) or in situations when your role involves questioning suspects and victims. Such people may not want to talk with you, at

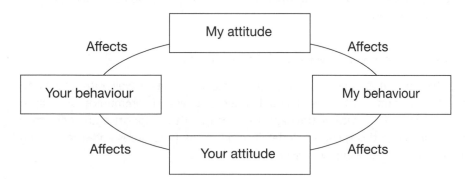

Figure 4.1 Betari's box

least initially, and so may be aggressive. It is important not to meet that aggression with aggression – but instead break the cycle of conflict. Through open posture and calm manner your behaviour and attitude can affect the other person's behaviour and subsequently calm them down. It therefore allows you, as a police officer, to act as an effective role model and demonstrate appropriate behaviour (Clements and Jones, 2002).

Therapeutic techniques are also important when working with victims and we will return to these techniques in the next section.

Interviewing victims

REFLECTIVE TASK

- *What do you think are the essential skills needed when dealing with victims? Make a list of some of those skills and then read this section.*

- *Once you have done that, visit www.westyorkshire.police.uk/?Page=188%7CPublic+ Satisfaction+and+Confidence, which details the figures of public confidence and satisfaction for West Yorkshire Police. What stands out in terms of the language used in the webpage?*

Increasing 'customer satisfaction' is becoming an important aspect of police work, so making a good impression with victims is now more crucial than ever. Under the Domestic Violence, Crime and Victims Act 2004, victims have a framework for making complaints against the police, while recent policy such as the victims' codes of practice (VCOPs) (2006) sets out the minimum standards that one can expect from the police. There has been a shift in power from police to victims in recent times, as the CJS becomes more concerned with customer satisfaction and confidence. As can be noted from the webpage in the last task, the language is focused around satisfaction and confidence, with victims labelled as 'customers'. Victims are now seen as consumers of a service, rather than people from whom to extract information. As Zedner notes:

> *The victim is now recognised as a key player in the criminal justice process . . . without the co-operation of the victim in reporting crime . . . most crime would remain unknown and unreported.*

(2002, p435)

Thus victims are now seen as centrally important within the CJS.

Now, more than ever, it is important for police officers to interact well with victims, to make a good impression and to have adequate interpersonal and communication skills in order to work successfully with victims and to offer them the support and advice they need. The remainder of this section will detail some of the procedures and interviewing skills that are needed for dealing with victims.

Working with (and not against) the victim

As mentioned in the section on interviewing suspects, therapeutic techniques can be very helpful for those doing police work, as they can help bolster police officers' interpersonal skills in person-to-person interactions and help them understand the psychology of human behaviour. In most psychotherapies the cornerstone of the work is the 'therapeutic alliance' – in other words, the working relationship between therapist and client (Claringbull, 2010). Without this relationship all other aspects of therapy are irrelevant. Therapeutic variables that have been linked to behaviour change, and personal growth are empathy, warmth, genuineness, respect, support, therapist's style and self-disclosure (Serran et al., 2003). All of this can be transposed to police work and can shore up the relationship between the police officer and the victim. Indeed, the same important relationship can be seen in the 'victim–police officer alliance'. This dyad is crucial for a variety of reasons, the main aspects being that a good working relationship means that the victim feels listened to and respected and so is more likely to work with the police. The victim is also more likely to have positive views of the police and feel positive about the future and overcoming the event. The victim–police officer alliance is therefore crucial and the following sections detail some of the techniques and skills necessary for satisfying this relationship.

The cognitive interview

The cognitive interview (CI) was designed as a way of minimising bias in eye-witness accounts and to improve recall in witness accounts (Geiselman, 1996). The approach to interviewing victims or witnesses draws on concepts from cognitive (how the memory works) and social psychology (what are good communications skills) and thus highlights an example of how psychology has practical relevance to policing.

The CI is based on memory research and theory, and consists of four retrieval mnemonics (tools that aid the memory) as follows.

- 'Mental reinstatement' of the personal and environmental context that existed at the time of the crime (Geiselman et al., 1985). This helps the person being interviewed to reinstate in their minds key aspects of the original event and so remember events with more clarity (Bull et al., 2006).

- 'Reporting everything' – this is about encouraging the victim to talk, as some people may hold back information because they feel it is not important. Victims or witnesses are encouraged to report partial information, regardless of the perceived importance of that information.

- 'Recounting the events in a variety of orders' – while approaching events in a chronological order may seem natural, other approaches should be used, for example going through the account in reverse order. Geiselman et al. (1985) encourage interviewers to work forward in time and backwards. Indeed, Geiselman et al. (1985) found that the technique can be beneficial in eliciting further additional information.

- 'Reporting the events from a variety of perspectives' encourages interviewees to recall the incident from a number of viewpoints; for example, try to place yourself in the role of a prominent character in the incident and think about what he or she may have seen (Geiselman et al., 1985).

The CI is well researched and studies have found that the procedure enhances both the quality and quantity of information recalled by witnesses compared with the standard police interview (Geiselman et al., 1985; Dando et al., 2008). Police officers are trained in the PEACE model of CI (see pages 42–3), which aims to give officers the skills necessary to interview witnesses and also adds components from the original CI (Fisher and Geiselman, 1992). The PEACE CI also includes establishing rapport, never guessing (so promoting free recall from the interviewee) and encouraging concentration (NSLEC, 2004). Dando et al. (2008) conducted a study on police officers' perceptions of the CI and their skills as interviewers. They found that establishing rapport, reporting everything, uninterrupted accounts and explaining the interview process were the most beneficial to police officers. Interestingly, two of these four components relate directly to good interpersonal and communication skills: the ability to establish rapport and explaining the interview (so that victims or witnesses are prepared). The rest of this section will focus on skills required by police officers for interviewing victims.

Interviewing and interpersonal skills

One of the key skills has already been mentioned as being crucial for interviewing victims and that is rapport. Developing rapport is critical in the interview setting; it can lower the defences of interviewees by putting them at ease and so obtain better quality information. Building rapport and maintaining it can help engage the victim and break down some of the barriers between interviewer and interviewee, which can lead to resistance. Having good rapport means that victims will feel safer talking about sensitive aspects of their crime and this will promote disclosure. As alluded to already, it is better to work with someone rather than against them. How can this be done? Police officers can do this by using interpersonal skills such as smiling, having an open posture and offering reassurance. There is a need to be mindful of context and not to be too formal and attempt to create a relaxed setting. This can create a sense for the victims that they are going to be working with someone who will take their views and feelings seriously (Gilbert, 1992).

Listening

The ability to listen is a key interpersonal and communication skill needed by police officers when interviewing victims. It is important that victims are given a voice and are heard. Giving victims this platform means that they are more likely to have a positive perception of the police and are more likely to cooperate with police enquiries (Stephens and Sinden, 2000).

> *[The ability to listen to] victims of crime can be one of the most useful things a supporter can do. Allowing people to describe their experience in their own words can help them to put it into perspective and begin to regain control of their lives.*
> (Sprackman, 2000, p13)

Listening, then, can empower victims and give them the encouragement to take back ownership of their lives. There are, however, two forms of listening: passive and active.

Active listening involves not just hearing the words and nodding in agreement in some passive way, but is about understanding what the person is saying and accepting it. To actively listen we must get inside the speaker, see things from their point of view and convey this to the listener (e.g. through reflection – 'it seems like you're saying this/that . . .') and understanding the meaning of what is being conveyed (Rogers and Farson, 1957). Indeed Rogers and Farson (1957) have found that, when people are actively listened to, personal change and growth can occur and they are more likely to move on from the event.

Empathy

Empathy can be seen as the ability to perceive accurately the feelings of another person and to communicate this with warmth (Sprackman, 2000). Forming an empathetic relationship can enable the victim to feel understood and accepted, and allow them to talk about painful experiences. This skill is particularly necessary for victims of violence and/or sexual assault (Gilbert, 1992). How do you do this? There are various ways to demonstrate empathy, including checking that you have interpreted what has been said in accordance with the victim's account, reflecting on the way you have communicated this and through being mindful of posture, tone and facial expression.

Genuineness

Genuineness is an interpersonal skill that can facilitate other skills and bring about change in others. It is achieved by being open with the speaker and responding in an honest manner (Sprackman, 2000). Through genuineness a person is accepted and can feel supported – a victim can feel that they matter and that they are not just a number. They are also more likely to have realistic expectations from the police, because the police officer has been 'real' with what can be done. Genuineness can also be thought of as congruence, which in this case means that the police officer is being him- or herself and is not presenting a façade; the officer is 'with the victim' at that time (and not mentally thinking about the next job, dealing with a handover package or trying to get away) (see, e.g., Rogers, 1956). How do you display genuineness? Police officers need to be honest and straightforward with their feelings. Being genuine is not about being a 'super supporter', but is about acknowledging the difficulty of the situation for the victim. Police officers need to be consistent with their verbal and non-verbal communication; for instance, ensure that you maintain good eye contact and have an open body posture.

Respect

The final interpersonal skill to be discussed, and arguably the most important, is respect. Respect underpins the other aforementioned interpersonal and communication skills, and is about accepting people for what and who they are without passing judgement. How do you demonstrate this? Value their thoughts, opinions and feelings without passing any moral judgement on the victims (refrain from victim blaming, e.g. what they did to put themselves in that position) (Sprackman, 2000). Try to ensure the right setting for a conversation and make sure it is one where the victim feels safe. One area where police officers can make a real difference is with initial interpersonal interaction and facilitating initial support with appropriate groups. It is useful to find extra information on both national and local support services that are out there for victims. As a local officer it is particularly important to have a knowledge of local force area support groups and charities. Through this knowledge you can support victims and refer them to effective groups. For instance, the group 'Surviving Trauma after Rape' (STAR) is a local charity in the West Yorkshire area that provides support, information and counselling to rape victims. Most victims will be unaware of this group, so information from an individual officer about this group could help recovery for a victim (see 'Useful websites' for more information on support groups; visit the websites and see what services they offer).

CASE STUDY

It is late on a Saturday night when you receive a call informing you of a disturbance. It is reported that a woman is saying that her husband has punched her and she further fears for her safety. The address is a familiar one. It is the home of Sarah and Simon Smith and this is the fifth call-out in four weeks.

A VIVID check tells you that Simon has been in trouble on numerous occasions for a variety of offences, including physical violence, criminal damage, threatening behaviour and public order offences. They both share council accommodation with their two young children. When you arrive at the house Sarah answers the door and you notice that she has significant bruising around her eye and the right side of her face. You walk into the house and, as you talk to Sarah, she becomes angry and starts shouting; it is clear she is upset.

During your interview Sarah struggles to stay calm and continually raises her voice; she becomes aggressive and demands that you 'lock him up'. She explains that she had been shopping at a local market and when she got back Simon was angry and questioned her about where she had been and what she had been doing. Despite the fact that the children were with her she says Simon believed she was seeing another man. He had been drinking and, during the argument, he hit her in the face a number of times while the children were present. She said she can no longer cope with the relationship and has also starting to drink heavily.

REFLECTIVE TASK

This type of case is one that you are likely to deal with as a police officer, and it is important in cases like this that you interact well with the victim, as it will have a lasting impression on her experiences with the police, on her decision to prosecute and on her recovery.

- *Read and reflect on the case study and then write down how you would interact with this victim and what interpersonal and communication skills you would draw on.*

C H A P T E R   S U M M A R Y

This chapter has outlined the key interpersonal and communication skills that are necessary for effective police work when dealing with suspects and victims. It has discussed and evaluated current procedures, such as the investigative interview process and the cognitive interview. It has also suggested how police officers' interactions can be more effective and constructive with victims by drawing on psychotherapeutic and psychological literature. As noted, interpersonal interactions with victims are the cornerstone of police work and it is increasingly crucial that victims are satisfied with the service provided by their police officer. Through an understanding and application of the core concepts outlined here (rapport, respect, genuineness and listening), police officers can be more effective in dealing with victims of crime.

REFERENCES

Bakker, AB and Heuven, E (2006) Emotional Dissonance, Burnout and In-role Performance among Nurses and Police Officers. *International Journal of Stress Management*, 13: 423–40.

Blagden, N (2011) Understanding Denial in Sexual Offenders: Implications for policy and practice. Unpublished PhD, Nottingham Trent University.

Bull, R, Cooke, C, Hatcher, R, Woodham, J, Bilby, C and Grant, T (2006) *Criminal Psychology: A beginners guide*. London: Oneworld.

Claringbull, N (2010) *What Is Counselling and Psychotherapy?* Exeter: Learning Matters.

Clements, P and Jones, J (2002) *The Diversity Training Handbook: A practical guide to understanding and changing attitudes*. London: Kogan Page.

Dando, C, Wilcock, R and Milne, R (2008) The Cognitive Interview: Inexperienced police officers' perceptions of their witness/victim interviewing practices. *Legal and Criminological Psychology*, 13(1): 59–70.

Fisher, RP and Geiselman, ER (1992) *Memory-enhancing Techniques for Investigative Interviewing: The cognitive interview*. Springfield, IL: Charles C Thomas.

Geiselman, RE (1996) *Eye Witness Testimony*. Balboa Island, CA: American College of Forensic Psychology Press.

Geiselman, RE, Fisher, RP, MacKinnon, DP and Holland, HL (1985) Eyewitness Memory Enhancement in the Police Interview: Cognitive retrieval mnemonics versus hypnosis. *Journal of Applied Psychology*, 70: 401–12.

Gilbert, N (1992) Realities and Mythologies of Rape. *Society*, 4: 4–10.

Gudjonsson, GH (2003) *The Psychology of Interrogations and Confessions: A handbook*. Chichester: John Wiley and Sons.

Gudjonsson, GH (2007) Investigative Interviewing, in Newburn, T, Williamson, T and Wright, A *Handbook of Criminal Investigation*. Cullompton: Willan.

Hollin, CR and Palmer, EJ (2006) Offending Behaviour Programmes: Controversies and resolutions, in Hollin, CR and Palmer, EJ (eds) *Offending Behaviour Programmes: Development, application and controversies*. Chichester: John Wiley and Sons.

Home Office (1992) *Principles of Investigative Interviewing*. Circular 22. London: Home Office.

Home Office (1993) *Training for Investigative Interviewing*. Circular 7. London: Home Office.

Mann, RE and Rollnick, S (1996) Motivational Interviewing With a Sex Offender Who Believed He Was Innocent. *Behavioural and Cognitive Psychotherapy*, 24: 127–34.

McCormack, T, Ashkar, A, Hunt, A, Change, E, Silberkleit, G and Geiselman, RE (2009) Indicators of Deception in an Oral Narrative: Which are more reliable? *American Journal of Forensic Psychiatry*, 30(4): 49–56.

Miller, WR (1996) Motivational Interviewing: Research, practice, and puzzles. *Addictive Behaviours*, 21(6): 835–42.

Miller, WR and Rollnick, S (2002) *Motivational Interviewing: Preparing people for change*. New York: Guilford Press.

NSLEC (National Specialist Law Enforcement Centre) (2004) *Practical Guide to Investigative Interviewing*. Wybosten: National Centre for Policing Excellence.

Rogers, CR (1956) The Necessary and Sufficient Conditions of Therapeutic Personality Change. *Journal of Consulting and Clinical Psychology*, 60(6): 827–32.

Rogers, CR and Farson, RE (1957) Active Listening, in Newman, RG, Danziger, MA and Cohen, M (eds) (1987) *Communication in Business Today*. Washington, DC: Heath and Company.

Salter, AC (2001) *Predators: Pedophiles, rapists and other sex offenders*. New York: Basic Books.

Serran, GA, Fernandez, Y, Marshall, WL and Mann, R (2003) Process Issues in Treatment: Application to sexual offender programmes. *Professional Psychology: Research and Practice*, 4, 368–74.

Sprackman, P (2000) *Helping People Cope with Crime*. London: Hodder.

Stephens, B and Sinden, P (2000) Victims' Voices: Domestic assault victims' perceptions of police demeanour. *Journal of Interpersonal Violence*, 15: 534–47.

Vrij, A (2000) *Detecting Lies and Deceit*. Chichester: John Wiley and Sons.

Vrij, A and Mann, S (2001) Telling and Detecting Lies in a High-stake Situation: The case of a convicted murderer. *Applied Cognitive Psychology*, 15: 187–203.

Vrij, A, Mann, S, Fisher, R, Leal, S, Milne, B and Bull, R (2008) Increasing Cognitive Load to Facilitate Lie Detection: The benefit of recalling an event in reverse order. *Law and Human Behavior*, 32: 253–65.

Walsh, DW and Milne, B (2008) Keeping the PEACE? A study of investigative interviewing practices in the public sector. *Legal and Criminological Psychology*, 13(1): 39–57.

Winter, D (2003) Stress in Police Officers: A personal construct theory perspective, in Horley, J (ed.) *Personal Construct Perspectives on Forensic Psychology*. Hove: Brunner-Routledge.

Zedner, L (2002) Victims, in Maguire, M, Morgan, R and Reiner, R (eds) *The Oxford Handbook of Criminology*. Oxford: University Press.

www.gasped.org.uk/index.php – Greater Awareness and Support for Parents Encountering Drugs (GASPED). GASPED is a registered charity established in 1995 offering information, advice, help, guidance, counselling, one-to-one appointments, respite and signposting group/peer support for the parents, partners, grandparents, families and carers who care for, or are affected by, a loved one using drugs and/or alcohol.

www.rapecrisis.org.uk – Rape Crisis (England and Wales) is a registered charity that supports the work of Rape Crisis Centres in England and Wales. It is a feminist organisation that promotes the needs of women and girls who have experienced sexual violence, in order to improve services provided for them, and works towards the elimination of sexual violence.

www.starproject.co.uk – The STAR (Surviving Trauma After Rape) Project is a free support service for females and males aged 14 and over who have been raped or sexually assaulted. STAR offers counselling and emotional and practical support throughout West Yorkshire. STAR Helpline: 01924 298954.

www.womensaid.org.uk – Women's Aid is the national domestic violence charity that helps up to **250,000** women and children every year. They run a 24-hour domestic violence helpline and work to end violence against women and children. They support over **500** domestic and sexual violence services across the country.

5 Investigative psychology and criminal profiling

Introduction

There is a large amount of literature published on offender profiling and on the efficacy of such approaches. The popularity of such approaches appears to go hand in hand with media dramas and the fictional depictions of what offender profilers do and what they are. Crime thrillers such as *Cracker* and *Crime Scene Investigations* (*CSI*) contribute to what has been termed the 'Hollywood effect' (Canter and Youngs, 2004) and the reality is somewhat different. These populist depictions only serve to perpetuate myths about the work of investigative psychologists and the role they play in criminal investigations. This chapter, however, demystifies this process and outlines the real purpose of offender profiling and its use within police investigations and police work. It also outlines the differences between investigative psychology and criminal profiling.

Criminal profiling has grown significantly over the years, particularly in the USA, following the opening of the Behavioural Science Unit by the FBI in the 1970s. It has been found that, between 1971 and 1981, the FBI provided profiling for 192 cases, although just a few years later this figure rose to 600 investigations. It is now believed that profiling is used in more than 1,000 cases. Criminal profiling has also been incorporated into investigations in the UK. For example, between 1981 and 1994, 29 profilers provided profiling assistance on 242 occasions (Snook et al., 2007). However, the evidence base for profiling, as is discussed in this chapter, still lags behind its current usage. Indeed, it could be contended that profiling has a legacy that overshadows its legitimacy. This chapter aims, then, to demystify the 'Hollywood effect' (Canter and Youngs, 2004) about profiling, which supports what Alison and Barrett (2004) call unrealistic views of the present state of profiling.

Criminal and offender profiling: background and overview

Offender profiling is the process of using the available information about a crime and crime scene to paint a psychological portrait of the unknown offender (Muller, 2000). In broad terms, it is the process of inferring characteristics of an offender based on an in-depth analysis of their crime(s). In essence, aspects of the offence, for example the crime scene, give us an insight or a 'psychological signature' that will tell us something meaningful about the offender's behaviour, motivations, personality and background (Farrington and Lambert, 2007). Thus, an offender profile can be thought of as a collection of psychological theories and techniques that attempt to draw inferences about an offender's characteristics by examining the crime scene (Alison et al., 2007). This particular form of profiling is mostly used in the USA and is different from what David Canter (2000) calls 'investigative psychology'. Although contents of offender profiles differ significantly, the following are usually included (see, e.g., Alison et al., 2007):

- perpetrator's ethnicity;
- perpetrator's gender;
- age range;
- marital status;
- employment;
- reaction to police questioning;

- degree of sexual maturity;

- likelihood of reoffending;

- previous similar offences;

- previous convictions.

The process of drawing inferences from crime scenes is by no means a new phenomenon, but an established aspect of crime fiction for over 200 years (Canter, 2000). We are all probably aware of Sir Arthur Conan Doyle's character of Sherlock Holmes and Agatha Christie's Hercule Poirot. Such characters make insightful deductions from crime scenes, picking out salient clues and drawing inferences about the offender's characteristics. The crime fiction depiction is usually of a man with a brilliant mind who can see things others cannot. Fast forward a few hundred years and such crime fiction is still as popular as ever, with TV shows depicting people 'getting into the minds of serial killers'. In some ways these dramatic representations reflect what police officers do on a daily basis, that is, making judgements and decisions based on the available information and evidence.

Perhaps the earliest criminal profile was conducted in the 1880s by a psychiatrist called Thomas Bond. Bond profiled the personality characteristics of an unknown serial killer who later became known as 'Jack the Ripper'. Bond, who was a police surgeon, noted the sexual aspects of the murders and made inferences about the perpetrator's age and his apparent hatred of women, which was demonstrated by extreme pre- and post-mortem injuries (Crighton, 2010). James Brussel profiled George Metesky, who was responsible for serial bomb explosions in New York between 1940 and 1956. Brussel suggested that the man (who later was identified as Metesky) would be a skilled mechanic from Connecticut and a Roman Catholic immigrant, and that he would have obsessional love for his mother, but hatred of his father. More specifically, Brussel went on to suggest that the bomber would be heavy, middle-aged and living with a sibling, and would have a personal vendetta against the city's power company. He also famously predicted that, when apprehended, he would be wearing a double-breasted suit buttoned to the top. The police tracked down Metesky who was a disgruntled ex-employee of the power company who, when told to get dressed by the police, returned wearing a fully fastened doubled-breasted suit jacket. The profile was extremely accurate with the only variation being that Metesky lived with two siblings and not one (Alison et al., 2007). These early examples have paved the way for the continued use of offender profiles, but just what are offender profiles and what is their evidence base?

Types of criminal profiling

Criminal investigative analysis

Since the 1970s investigators at the FBI's Behavioural Science Unit (BSU) have assisted local and national law enforcement agencies in narrowing investigations by providing criminal personality profiles (Douglas et al., 1986). The BSU is now the Behavioural Analysis Unit, which is a part of the National Center for Analysis of Violent Crime (NCAVC). The NCAVC provides behaviour-based operational support to federal, state, local and international law enforcement agencies involved in the investigation of unusual or repetitive violent crimes, as well as other matters of interest to law enforcement and national security agencies (see in 'Useful websites'). Profiling has been used in a variety of settings and for a variety of offenders, for example hostage takers, child abductors, murderers and rapists. The main rationale behind criminal investigative analysis (CIA) is that behaviour reflects personality, and by examining behaviour the investigator may be able to determine what type of person is responsible for the offence (Douglas et al., 1986). There also seems to be an underlying cognitive-behavioural element to CIA in that NCAVC's criminal profiling approach is partly based on the way a person thinks (their mindset) directing their behaviour. In other words, *it is a technique for identifying the major personality and behavioural characteristics of an individual based upon an analysis of the crimes he or she has committed* (Douglas et al., 1986, p405).

As noted, crime scene analysis/CIA infers behaviour and personality from the crime scene, thus narrowing the field of suspects and aiding in the likely apprehension of an offender (Beauregard, 2010). CIA has generated typologies of offenders and perhaps the best known and most influential distinction is that between 'organised' and 'disorganised' homicide offenders (Crighton, 2010). Although originally applied to just murderers, this has been expanded to rapists and arsonists, with rape being the second most profiled crime after murder (Dowden et al., 2007; Crighton, 2010). The organised/disorganised model of offence behaviour assumes that each offender type has a distinct modus operandi (MO) when committing a crime, and that crime scene characteristics and offender characteristics will differ between the two groups. Tables 5.1 and 5.2 are originally from Alison et al. (2007, pp495–6) and are adapted from Burgess et al. (1985).

Criminal profilers have also attempted to create offender typologies as a way of categorising offenders and aiding with investigation. While most of the research has focused on rapists and serial murderers, investigative psychology has also been used to examine burglars. Salter (2001) argues that there are different types of rapists; there are some who are opportunistic, some who are compulsive, some who will seek out strangers, and others who will rape women only known to them. The heterogeneity in rapists has led some authors to create typologies of such offenders, which have been used by many

Table 5.1 Crime scene characteristics

Organised	Disorganised
Planned offence	Spontaneous offence
Controlled conversation	Minimal conversation
Scene reflects control	Scene is random and sloppy
Demands submissive victim	Sudden violence to victim
Restraints used	Minimal use of restraints
Aggressive prior to death	Sex after death
Body hidden	Body left in view
Weapon/evidence absent	Weapon/evidence present
Transports victim	Body left at scene

Table 5.2 *Organised and disorganised offender characteristics*

Organised	Disorganised
High intelligence	Low intelligence
Socially adequate	Socially inadequate
Sexually competent	Sexually inexperienced
Lives with father	Unskilled occupation
High birth order	Low birth order
Harsh discipline	Harsh/inconsistent discipline
Controlled mood	Anxious mood
Charming	Minimal use of alcohol during crime
Situational cause	Lives alone
Geographically mobile	Lives/works near crime scene
Occupationally mobile	Significant behaviour change
Follows media	Little interest in media
Model prisoner	Poor personal hygiene
Masculine image	Usually doesn't date
	High-school dropout

offender profilers. The following typology is based on Knight and Prentky (1990), as detailed by Langton and Marshall (2001) (although it is not exclusive).

- **Opportunistic** – Offences are unplanned and impulsive, with the goal being immediate sexual gratification.

- **Pervasively angry** – The offence is an instance of poor behavioural control. The degree of force and violence used is excessive and brutal. Resistance from the victim is likely to exacerbate violence.

- **Sexual** – The sexual type can be subdivided into two categories: sadistic and non-sadistic. The sexual aggression of the sadistic rapist is manifested in the humiliation of the victim and the infliction of physical harm. Non-sadistic rapists are characterised by having an enduring sexual preoccupation, with the offence occurring through the manifestation of deviant sexual interests.

- **Vindictive** – This type of rapist shares the characteristics of aggression and force with the pervasively angry rapist, but anger is not part of a general disposition; instead, it is specifically targeted at women. There is a *sexual component in the assault behaviour but the aggression is not eroticized, suggesting that paraphilic fantasies are not involved* (Langton and Marshall, 2001, p505).

There have been other types of rapist identified, but the consistent finding is that there do appear to be differences in the use of force, motivation, socialisation, victim empathy and deviant sexual interest. For example, in line with serial murderers' profiles, there have been found to be two 'power-type' rapists: power-assertive and power-reassurance. The power-assertive rapist believes that men should dominate women and that he is entitled to sex whenever he wants. He will be a selfish individual and, during the offence, will be concerned with his own sexual gratification (Carney, 2004). The power-reassurance rapist will suffer from feelings of inadequacy. Therefore, his offending will be a way to reassure himself of his own masculinity and dominance over women. This type of rapist would use a minimal amount of force in the offence because he would want the victim to desire him. He will fantasise that the victim will enjoy the offence and will want to do it again voluntarily (Carney, 2004). However, it could be argued that this simply forms part of the excuse-making discourse, rather than actually highlighting key differences between the offenders.

There have also been influential typologies for serial killers that have been used extensively in CIA profiling. Holmes and Holmes (1996) outline five types of serial killer – visionary, mission, lust, thrill, power/control – along with their crime scene actions. This typology has been very influential for FBI profilers. Table 5.3 provides an outline of the different types of

Table 5.3 Types of serial killer and their organisation and crime scene actions

Type of serial killer	Organised/disorganised	Modus operandi
Visionary	Disorganised	Belongings and clothing scattered
		Weapon left in victim
		Weapon of opportunity
		Trail of clothing from the crime scene
		Bludgeoned
		Psychotic
Mission	Disorganised	Bludgeoned
		Firearm use
		Murder weapon missing
		Throat cut
Lust	Organised	Multiple crime scenes
		Multiple sex acts – may include vaginal and object penetration
		Mutilations – vaginal, abdominal, thoracic
Thrill	Organised	Torture
		Body concealed
		Alive during sex acts
		Multiple crime scenes
		Ligature and manual strangulation
		Bite marks
		Tampered with evidence
Power/control	Organised	Multiple crime scenes
		Restraints and torture
		Beaten and cuts
		Decapitation
		Burns on victim
		Body concealed and body parts missing

Source: Adapted from Holmes and Holmes (1996) and Canter et al. (2004).

serial killer, their organisation and their MOs. There are some similarities to the rapist profiles above.

'Visionary' killers differ from the other serial killers in that they seem to have lost touch with reality. Their violent actions and killings are related to their auditory hallucinations that compel them to kill. Their delusions and hallucinations direct the killer to murder similar individuals. For instance, a killer may only kill women who are prostitutes; for example, Peter Sutcliffe (the 'Yorkshire Ripper') claimed he heard voices when killing prostitutes (Webber, 2010). The 'mission' serial killer is focused on the murder itself. He is compelled to murder in order to rid the world of a certain category of people he has decided are unworthy (Canter and Wentink, 2004). The 'mission' serial killer is not psychotic, unlike the visionary. The 'lust' serial killer kills for sexual gratification, which is the focal point of the murder even once the victim is dead. They will spend a lot of time planning the murder and will take pleasure from the process of the murderous event (Canter and Wentink, 2004). The 'thrill' serial killer murders for the pleasure and excitement of killing. Once the victim is dead, this murderer loses interest. This type of killing often involves a long process including extended acts of torture (Canter and Wentink, 2004). 'Power/control' killers also derive sexual pleasure from the act, but also from controlling and destroying life, thus sexual gratification is not necessarily the focal point. The motives stem from the dominance of another human being (Webber, 2010).

There are, however, criticisms of these different typologies/categories in that they are too descriptive and simplistic. Canter et al. (2004) are critical of the long-standing assumption that serial killers can be neatly categorised into disorganised and organised killers, and in their study found that aspects of both can co-occur and that it is likely murderers will contain aspects of both. They contend that all serial killings will probably have a recognisable organised quality to them (given that they form a series of similar vicious crimes). Canter et al. (2004) are also critical of much of the criminal profiling literature on crime scene actions and instead argue for what they call 'investigative psychology' (this will be discussed in more detail later in this chapter).

CASE STUDY

A young woman's nude body was discovered at 3 p.m. on the roof of an apartment building, where it was determined that she was killed at 6.30 a.m. The victim was a resident of the apartment block and was on her way to work before being attacked in her apartment block. She had been badly beaten and was strangled with the strap of her bag, although marks around her neck suggest this was first attempted by hand. The cause of death was asphyxia caused by strangulation.

The woman was found with numerous post-mortem injuries (inflicted after death), including bite marks on her inner thighs, severed nipples (probably with a pocket penknife), multiple fractures to her face and jaw, and objects inserted into her vagina. The victim was also found with her underwear pulled over her head and writing on her body, which read 'You can't stop me.' She wore a crucifix around her neck, but this was absent from the body and presumed taken by the offender. Although no semen was found in the vagina it was found on the body, suggesting that the offender masturbated over the victim. The victim was left in a provocative and humiliating position.

(Based on Douglas et al., 1986, pp415–16)

PRACTICAL TASK

- *Attempt to create a profile of the offender in the above case study based on what has been covered so far in this chapter. Elicit the most salient aspects of the case to draw up a picture of the offender. Consider their employment status, education, age, whether they are organised or disorganised, characteristics of the perpetrator (the type of killer), degree of sexual maturity and their likelihood of reoffending.*

- *Once you have created your profile of the offender, think about how useful this profile might be to police officers. Now consider the potential problems the use of such a profile might cause. We'll revisit this later with the profile from Douglas et al. (1986).*

Investigative psychology

Investigative psychology *covers all aspects of psychology that are relevant to the conduct of criminal and civil investigations* (Canter, 2000, p1091). Canter and Youngs (2004) argue that profiling needs to develop into a scientific discipline if it is to contribute effectively to police investigations. For Canter (2010), investigative psychology is based on empirically sound psychological principles rather than on the more anecdotally based processes of offender profiling commonly associated with CIA. The process of investigative psychology can be broken down into three aspects: the scientific study of investigation information (its retrieval, evaluation and utilisation); the inferences that can be made about criminal activity (based on sound empirical principles); and police actions and decisions (how they can be supported and improved) (see Figure 5.1). For instance, investigative psychology can be useful for police officers in terms of identifying the important characteristics of the offence and the offender. This could be through the production of crime maps showing the location of specific crimes or providing data on the relative commonness or rarity of that crime or action, which can be used to draw sound inferences (Canter, 2010).

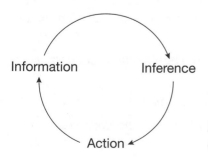

Figure 5.1 Investigation cycle giving rise to the field of investigative psychology (based on Canter (2010))

While investigative psychology covers all aspects of psychology that are relevant to the conduct of criminal or civil investigations, one of its main focuses is on the ways criminal activities may be examined and understood in order for the detection of crime to be improved. As such, it aims to be important in the investigative decision-making process. So, in order for inferences about a potential offender to be of value, they must relate to things that police officers can actually act on. This could be information about where the offender may be living or likely locations for the next offence (Canter and Youngs, 2004). However, as Canter and Youngs (2004) argue, deep psychodynamic interpretations of the offender's motivations are likely to be of less value to police officers. They point out that the police were able to arrest and convict Barry George, the man who had been thought to be responsible for Jill Dando's death, without any clear ideas as to why he committed the crime (though we have to think seriously about the merits of this argument given that he was later acquitted of this crime). Thus, Canter and Youngs (2004) would argue that populist explanations of offender motivations, which are not grounded in evidence, are not useful in helping catch criminals. Profiles are only of value if they facilitate the detective decision-making process.

Investigative psychology has suffered from similar criticisms to CIA in that it is only as good as the data it is based on (i.e. if the data from secondary sources is unreliable, so will be the inferences made by the investigative psychologist). Some have even suggested that it does not bring anything additional to the table, just offers new avenues to explore. However, investigative psychology is the scientific application of psychology to real-world problems that are of benefit in the applied criminal justice world (Muller, 2000). It then seeks to avoid conjecture and unscientific approaches to criminal behaviour.

CASE STUDY REVISITED

Earlier in this chapter you were asked to create a profile for a case study (see pages 60–1). Douglas et al. (1986, p419) provided a profile for this case; see if you were able to pick out some of the key features.

Douglas et al.'s (1986) profile suggested the following.

- *The killer would be a white male, aged between 25 and 30, of average appearance and of average intelligence, but he would be a high school or college dropout.*

- *He might be unemployed or employed in blue-collar work and would have no military history.*

- *Alcohol and drugs would not play a major role because of the time of the offence.*

- *He would be familiar to the context and there would be a reason for the killer to be there at 6.30 a.m. – he could live in the apartment complex, work there or be on business there.*

- *He may have preferred the victim conscious but had to render her unconscious because he didn't want to be discovered.*

- *He would be sexually inexperienced, inadequate and never married.*

- *He would have a pornography collection and he would have sadistic tendencies.*

- *The sexual acts showed controlled aggression, but a rage against or hatred of women.*

- *The murderer's infliction of sexual, sadistic acts on an inanimate body suggests he was disorganised.*

- *He would be a very confused person and may have had previous mental problems.*

- *The crime scene revealed that the killer felt justified in his actions and that he felt no remorse.*

- *He left the body exactly how he wanted it to be found.*

- *The messages on the body indicate that he may kill again.*

REFLECTIVE TASK

- *What do you think of this profile? Does it match with yours? Do you think it is vague or specific?*

- *Now you have read about investigative psychology and criminal profiling, how would you compare the two? Which do you prefer and why?*

Geographical profiling

Investigative psychology is related to, and is influenced by, geographical profiling and both aim to identify the likely area of an offender's residence from the location of the crime (Bull et al., 2006). However, considering the environment and spatial locality of crimes is nothing new to policing or criminology. Early theories from the 'Chicago school' of criminology focused on the internal spatial and social structure of cities (Ashby and Craglia, 2007). Burgess's concentric zones theory, for example, postulated that crime was located in the inner-city areas and became less concentrated and problematic the further away from the city centre.

One of the main theories within geographical profiling is the principle of 'distance decay'. This is based on the hypothesis that, if someone wants something, they will only travel as far as they need to in order to obtain it. Thus, if offenders are presented with two victims to offend against, they are more likely to choose the one that is geographically closer to them (Bull et al., 2006).

The criminological theories of 'rational choice' and 'routine activities' are also important in geographical profiling. In the rational choice perspective, the decision-making process of offenders and their choice to commit the crime occurs because crime is perceived as the most adequate way of achieving the desired benefits, for example sexual gratification (Beauregard and LeClerc, 2007). However, the decision to offend is seldom based on one decision and will often depend on situational cues, for example the victim may be alone in a park (desired location for offence), but interaction with a bystander will mean that the offender will have to reassess the situation or not commit the offence. As such, Beauregard and LeClerc (2007) argue that sexual offending is based on 'premeditated opportunism', where the offending scenario gives way to situational cues, which trigger the offence.

This links with routine activities theory, which is based on an interrelationship between a motivated offender (e.g. rapist, burglar), absence of a capable guardian (e.g. no CCTV, no one being around, victim alone in park) and suitable target (e.g. victim type, empty property etc.). Cohen and Felson (1979) argued that crime occurs when all three conditions are met, for example when there is a motivated offender, when there is a suitable target and when there is an absence of capable guardians.

Canter and Larkin's (1993) 'circle theory of environmental range' suggests that the rapist's location could be predicted if you identify the two offences that are furthest from each other and then draw a circle around them. The residence of the offender will be in that circle and more than likely in the middle. Canter and Larkin (1993) found in his study that most offenders located their crimes within the circular region. However, there has been little empirical follow-up work and the offender's offending is likely to vary depending on the type of crime and their motivation (Bull et al., 2006).

Geographical profiling is becoming increasingly popular and useful to the police. The increased use of geographic information systems (GIS) and crime mapping allows information about crime locations to be systematically analysed and can help with the efficient allocation of police resources. Geographical profiling can then contribute to intelligence-led policing and to overall force strategy and performance by allowing the police to target problem environments and evaluate whether certain operations have been effective. This can also allow a comparison between the rates of specific crimes at different time points (Ashby and Craglia, 2007). There has been much more public dissemination from the police of crime maps and hotspots and it can be a good way of informing the public about where crimes are taking place (so the public can be extra vigilant) and also showing how effective (or ineffective) the police are being at tackling local problems.

PRACTICAL TASK

Visit www.police.uk and investigate the geographical statistics of different crimes for your area. Then consider the advantages and disadvantages of the availability of this information for this public and the police.

Criminal profiling: evidence base

We now have a better understanding of the different types of criminal profiling, how they can be utilised by police investigators, and the different typologies of certain offenders. But how reliable and useful are criminal profiles for police investigators? And what do the police think of criminal profiles? Snook et al. (2007) conducted a meta-analysis to investigate whether the published literature on profiling used common-sense rationales (e.g. intuition; 'tell it like it is') or whether it was based on empirical (scientifically testable) rationales, that is whether it had a reliable basis. It was found that common-sense rationales, those not based on scientifically derived principles, have flourished, which is concerning as it opens up the possibility of error. They found that a large proportion of the studies in the USA (where crime scene analysis/CIA is more prominent) were based on common-sense rationales and not based on empirical research. This led Snook et al. (2007) to argue that, at present, the technique is redundant for criminal investigations. Indeed, evidence on whether professional profilers outperform non-profilers is mixed and, while they may be marginally more accurate, Snook et al. (2008) argue that there is no compelling scientific evidence to support the positive view of criminal profiling that dominates our popular opinion. Indeed, far from being a cutting-edge science, criminal profiling approaches are based on typologies that lack empirical support and are often based on an outdated understanding of human behaviour.

There also needs to be an air of caution when interrupting the criminal profile as there is the potential for misdirection in the police investigation and the ambiguity of the profile may lead to some over-interpretation. Indeed, clinical and personality psychological research has consistently demonstrated that people are inclined to accept ambiguous, vague and general statements as accurate descriptions of themselves and their personalities (Snook et al., 2008). This is sometimes referred to as the 'Forer effect' or 'Barnum effect'. In Forer's (1949) study he conducted an experiment where students were told they could have a personality test and assessment (when in fact they were given a list of ambiguous statements) and were then asked to rate how accurate the personality test was. The test contained statements such as 'you have a great need for others to like and admire you', 'you have a great deal of unused capacity', 'disciplined and self-controlled outside, you tend to be worrisome and insecure inside.' Forer (1949) found that the personality test received a high level of personal validation; in short, people believed it. We can see the same sort of ambiguous statements in the profile we saw earlier. For instance, 'he may be unemployed or employed in blue-collar work', 'average intelligence . . . very confused and may have suffered from previous mental health problems', 'he could live, work or be on business in the apartment complex'. The key to these statements is that we can add the tag phrase 'or not', for example, 'he could live in the apartment . . . or not'. The statements are suitably vague, could be attributable to many people and are the characteristics that are most common in criminals aged between 25 and 35, e.g. high school dropouts, unemployed and so on. These statements are relatively unremarkable and probably wouldn't help narrow down a list of suspects. Interestingly, there is evidence of the 'Forer effect' in criminal profiles.

Alison et al. (2003) examined the extent to which police officers perceived ambiguous statements as accurately representing an offender in a case. The study comprised two groups of police officers, both groups receiving the same crime details and bogus criminal profile, although one group was given the real offender characteristics and the other group a fabricated offender (whose characteristics were the contrast of the other offender). Both groups rated the profiles as somewhat accurate; interestingly, 40 per cent of those in group A (genuine offender) rated the profile as generally very accurate while 50 per cent of group B rated it as very accurate. The results highlight that police officers are prepared to accept ambiguous statements as comprising an accurate profile (i.e. are likely to overinterpret so that the profile fits the offender) and that any profile could describe an offender. This is worrying as it could mislead an investigation and is linked with investigative psychology's critique of CIA as being unscientific.

However, when looking at how effective and useful criminal profiles are for criminal investigations we need to ask the police and criminal investigators for their opinions. Copson (1995) found in his study that 82.6 per cent of police officers thought that criminal profiling was operationally useful and over 90 per cent said they would use criminal profiling advice in the future. Trager and Brewster (2001) also found that police investigators believed that criminal profiling was useful, particularly in guiding the inter-rogations of the suspect and criminal investigation, but not necessarily for identifying the suspect. Furthermore, Torres et al. (2006) looked at the perceptions of forensic psycho-logists and psychiatrists on the utility of criminal profiles. They found that, while 25 per cent thought criminal profiling was unreliable, the majority of respondents, 86 per cent, thought that profiling was useful to law enforcement and supported further research. It is clear that practitioners do find merit in traditional criminal profiling and believe it is of use.

What about investigative psychology? While investigative psychology has produced testable hypotheses about criminal behaviour that are relevant to police investigations, the approach still lacks empirical support and there are few studies that have tested its efficacy. Unlike CIA, it is based on testable theories such as spatial patterns of serial murderers, crime circle theory and the situational and environmental aspects of offenders. Studies from an investigative psychology approach have some clear implications for profiling, as they can suggest strategies for narrowing down the range of potential suspects (Muller, 2000) and predicting the likelihood of where they will reside. The paradigm has also been heavily critical of US criminal profiling and some of the taken-for-granted assumptions and common-sense rationales on which, investigative psychologists would argue, it is based. It could also be argued that criminal profilers are guilty of something akin to the fundamental attribution error, namely being too focused on dispositional traits in explaining behaviour rather than acknowledging the situational and environmental elements. Situational factors contribute as much as personality dispositions to the prediction of behaviour (Snook et al., 2008). It is clear that, for both crime scene analysis/CIA and investigative psychology, more investigation and evaluation is needed, although investigative psychology is based on an empirically testable basis and produces testable hypotheses to back up its claims (Muller, 2000).

Policing practice and practical problems

As highlighted already there are some real issues with the evidence base of offender profiling in general and with the specific methodologies (e.g. CIA and investigative psychology). There are also further practical problems that can hinder an accurate offender profile. Most profilers (UK and USA) have not been police officers and do not have first-hand experience of criminal investigation. Most have also never been to a crime scene, hence many of the techniques come from secondary sources (White, 2010). This can be a reliability issue, as most profilers are reliant on inferring things about a potential offender based on secondary sources. It is important to remember that offender profiles should be seen as part of a police investigation officer's toolkit and not as the endgame. While profiling is still utilised by the police and agencies like the FBI, there are still insufficient data and published figures to detail their accuracy (this should be the yardstick by which we measure profiles) (Muller, 2000). While it has been suggested that between 75 and 80 per cent are accurate (see, e.g., Ressler and Shachtman, 1992; White, 2010), there is little evidence to support such claims. However, even if such claims were corroborated, 75 per cent accuracy is not good enough for the courts. This makes the implications for profiling and using profiles clear. If a profile is wrong or even marginally inaccurate, police may be misled, which could lead to the offender remaining undetected for longer or increase the chances of innocent people being accused (and possibly convicted). Indeed, there are cases where profiles have been used to convict a person and later the person has been found innocent on appeal. The case of Timothy Masters serves as a warning beacon for those reliant on offender profiles.

CASE STUDY

Picking up pieces: the potential misuse of offender profiles

Timothy Masters was convicted of the murder of Peggy Hettrick and the sexual mutilation of her body. He was sentenced to life in prison without parole. However, he was convicted almost exclusively on a profile of a highly respected forensic psychologist (who had never met or spoken to Timothy Masters) and his testimony. Nine years later Timothy Masters was released following a successful appeal, as DNA evidence proved that he did not commit the offence.

REFLECTIVE TASK

- *What are the potential pitfalls of using offender profiles?*
- *What could the police have done in order to obtain a more accurate profile in this case?*

A further practical issue is whether offender profilers assume too much similarity between offenders; that is, is there too much an assumption that one particular offender will behave similarly to another offender with the same MO. This point is related to distinctions made earlier about certain offender types, for example whether they are organised or disorganised. Furthermore, conventional approaches to offender profiling assume a homology of the characteristics of offenders with their crime scene actions (Mokros and Alison, 2002). A study by Mokros and Alison (2002) tested the homology hypothesis on a group of convicted rapists (n=100) and found no evidence of homology between crime scene actions and background characteristics in the sample. This has particular impact on profiles as most contain salient characteristics such as socio-economic status, age, marital status and organised vs. disorganised (White, 2010). In the USA, the FBI approach to offender profiling rests somewhat on the assumption that behaviour reflects personality (e.g. the crime scene reflects mindset and personality): *The crime scene is presumed to reflect the murderer's behavior and personality in much the same way as furnishings reveal the homeowner's character* (Douglas et al., 1992, p21). Think about this for a moment – does your home (its furnishings and presentation etc.) reflect your personality? Would it be reasonable for someone to assume your mindset from your home? Perhaps it would be, although perhaps you rent a house that is fully furnished, or you haven't got the money to furnish your place how you want, or you are going through a bit of a transition and so perhaps your house is more of a mess than usual. While it has been found that profilers are better at identifying offenders than non-profilers (see, e.g., Pinizzotto and Finkel, 1990) (although some studies have found no significant differences), there seem to be some inherent problems with inferring personality from crime scene behaviour.

CHAPTER SUMMARY

This chapter has aimed to demystify and 'de-Hollywoodise' populist notions of criminal profiling, has suggested that there are deficits in criminal profiling and has highlighted some of the potential pitfalls for police investigators. However, if the measure of something can be found in customer satisfaction, criminal profiling would seem to be useful. Police seem to think that offender profiles are useful in the investigative process, but that they are limited and not to be relied upon. Indeed, there is a real lack of empirical support for criminal investigation analysis and it has been argued that it has the potential to mislead investigations and that it is based on common-sense principles. Investigative psychology has also been detailed and discussed, and it has been highlighted that it takes a serious scientific approach to all aspects of the crime investigative process. That said, and despite an empirical grounding, there is little evidence that investigative psychology outperforms crime scene analysis/CIA or that it has utility over and above it. While investigative psychology appears the way forward for police officers, more research is needed on its utility and efficacy.

FURTHER READING

Canter, D (2000) Investigative Psychology, in Siegel, JA, Saukko, PJ and Knupfer, GC (eds.) *Encyclopedia of Forensic Sciences*, vol. 3. New York: Academic Press.

Canter, D (2010) Investigative Psychology, in Brown, JM and Campbell, EA (eds) *The Cambridge Handbook of Forensic Psychology*. Cambridge: Cambridge University Press.

Trager, J and Brewster, J (2001) The Effectiveness of Psychological Profiles. *Journal of Police and Criminal Psychology*, 16(1): 20–8.

REFERENCES

Alison, L and Barrett, E (2004) The Interpretation and Utilisation of Offender Profiles: A critical review of 'traditional' approaches to profiling, in Adler, JR (ed.) *Forensic Psychology: Concepts, debates and practice*. Cullompton: Willan.

Alison, L, Smith, M and Morgan, K (2003) Interpreting the accuracy of offender profiles. *Psychology, Crime & Law*, 9: 185–95.

Alison, L, McLean, C and Almond, L (2007) Profiling Suspects, in Newburn, T, Williamson, T and Wright, A (eds) *Handbook of Criminal Investigation*. Cullompton: Willan.

Ashby, D and Craglia, M (2007) Profiling Places: Geodemographics and GIS, in Newburn, T, Williamson, T and Wright, A (2007) *Handbook of Criminal Investigation*. Cullompton: Willan.

Beauregard, E (2010) Rape and Sexual Assault in Investigative Psychology: The contribution of sex offenders' research to offender profiling. *Journal of Investigative Psychology and Offender Profiling*, 7(1): 1–13.

Beauregard, E and LeClerc, B (2007) An Application of the Rational Choice Approach to the Offending Process of Sex Offenders: A closer look at the decision-making. *Sexual Abuse: A Journal of Research and Treatment*, 19(2): 115–33.

Bull, R, Cooke, C, Hatcher, R, Woodham, J, Bilby, C and Grant, T (2006) *Criminal Psychology: A beginners guide*. London: Oneworld Publications.

Burgess, J, Douglas, J and Ressler, R (1985) Classifying Sexual Homicide Crime Scenes. *FBI Law Enforcement Bulletin*, 54: 12–17.

Canter, D (2000) Investigative Psychology, in Siegel, JA, Saukko, PJ and Knupfer, GC (eds) *Encyclopedia of Forensic Sciences*, vol. 3. New York: Academic Press.

Canter, D (2010) Investigative Psychology, in Brown, JM and Campbell, EA (eds) *The Cambridge Handbook of Forensic Psychology*. Cambridge: Cambridge University Press.

Canter, D and Larkin, P (1993) The Environmental Range of Serial Rapists. *Journal of Environmental Psychology*, 13: 63–69.

Canter, D and Wentink, N (2004) An Empirical Test of Holmes and Holmes's Serial Murder Typology. *Criminal Justice and Behavior*, 20: 1–26.

Canter, D and Youngs, D (2004) Beyond Offender Profiling: The need for an investigative psychology, in Bull, R and Carson, D (eds) *Handbook of Psychology in Legal Contexts*, 2nd edition. Chichester: John Wiley and Sons.

Canter, DV, Alison, LJ, Alison, E and Wentick, N (2004) The Organised/Disorganised Typology of Serial Murder: Myth or model? *Psychology, Public Policy, and Law*, 10(3): 293–320.

Carney, TP (2004) *Practical Investigation of Sex Crimes: A strategic and operational approach*. Boca Raton, FL: CRC Press.

Cohen, LE and Felson, M (1979) Social Change and Crime Rate Trends: A routine activity approach. *American Sociological Review*, 44: 588–608.

Copson, G (1995) *Coals to Newcastle? Part 1: A study of offender profiling*. London: Home Office, Police Research Group.

Crighton, D (2010) Offender Profiling, in Towl, GJ and Crighton, DA (eds) *Forensic Psychology*. Chichester: BPS Blackwell.

Douglas, JE, Ressler, RK, Burgess, AW and Hartman, CR (1986) Criminal Profiling from Crime Scene Analysis. *Behavioral Sciences and the Law*, 4, 401–21.

Douglas, JE, Burgess, AW, Burgess, AG and Ressler, RK (1992) *Crime Classification Manual: A standard system for investigating and classifying violent crime*. New York: Simon and Schuster.

Dowden, C, Bennell, C and Bloomfield, S (2007) Advances in Offender Profiling: A systematic review of the profiling literatures published over the past 30 years. *Journal of Police and Criminal Psychology*, 22: 44–56.

Farrington, DP and Lambert, S (2007) Predicting Offender Profiles from Offense and Victim Characteristics. *Criminal Profiling*, 2: 135–67.

Forer, B (1949) The Fallacy of Personal Validation: A classroom demonstration of gullibility. *Journal of Abnormal and Social Psychology*, 44: 118–23.

Holmes, RM and Holmes, S (1996) *Profiling Violent Crimes: An investigative tool.* Thousand Oaks, CA: Sage.

Knight, RA and Prentky, RA (1990) Classifying Sexual Offenders: The development and corroboration of taxonomic models, in Marshall, WL, Laws, DR and Barbaree, HE (eds) *Handbook of Sexual Assault: Issues, theories, and treatment of the offender.* New York: Plenum.

Langton, CM and Marshall, WL.(2001) Cognition in Rapists: Theoretical patterns by typological breakdown. *Aggression and Violent Behaviour*, 6: 499–518.

Mokros, A and Alison, L (2002) Is Offender Profiling Possible? Testing the predicted homology of crime scene actions and background characteristics in a sample of rapists. *Legal and Criminological Psychology*, 7: 25–43.

Muller, DA (2000) Criminal Profiling: Real science or just wishful thinking? *Homicide Studies*, 4: 234–64.

Pinizzotto, AJ and Finkel, NJ (1990) Criminal Personality Profiling: An outcome and process study. *Law and Human Behavior*, 14: 215–33.

Ressler, RK and Shachtman, T (1992) *Whoever Fights Monsters.* New York: Pocket Books.

Salter, A (2001) *Predators, Paedophiles, Rapists and Other Sex Offenders.* New York: Basic Books.

Snook, B, Eastwood, J, Gendreau, P, Goggin, C and Cullen, RM (2007) Taking Stock of Criminal Profiling: A narrative review and meta-analysis. *Criminal Justice and Behavior*, 34: 437–53.

Snook, B, Cullen, RM, Bennell, C, Taylor, PJ and Gendreau, P (2008) The Criminal Profiling Illusion: What's behind the smoke and mirrors? *Criminal Justice and Behavior*, 35(10): 1257–1276.

Torres, AN, Boccaccini, MT and Miller, HA (2006) Perceptions of the Validity and Utility of Criminal Profiling among Forensic Psychologists and Psychiatrists. *Professional Psychology: Research and Practice*, 37: 51–8.

Trager, J and Brewster, J (2001) The Effectiveness of Psychological Profiles. *Journal of Police and Criminal Psychology*, 16(1): 20–8.

Webber, C (2010) *Psychology and Crime.* London: Sage.

White, JH (2010) Using Criminal Investigative Analysis, paper presented at the American College of Forensic Psychology 26th Annual Symposium, San Francisco, CA.

USEFUL WEBSITES

www.fbi.gov/about-us/cirg/investigations-and-operations-support/investigations-operations-support – FBI information on their National Center for Analysis of Violent Crime (NCAVC) and its Behavioural Analysis Units

www.ia-ip.org – International Academy for Investigative Psychology

www.i-psy.com – Centre for Investigative Psychology

6 Victims and the psychological consequences of victimisation

CHAPTER OBJECTIVES

By the end of this chapter you should be able to:

- understand the different types of victims and the range of effects criminal victimisation has on them;
- appreciate the psychological consequences of victimisation;
- be mindful of the role effective police work can have on victim satisfaction, police confidence and initial recovery.

LINKS TO STANDARDS

This chapter provides opportunities for links with the following Skills for Justice, National Occupational Standards (NOS) for Police and Law Enforcement 2008.

BE2 (CJC102)   Provide initial support to victims, survivors and witnesses, and assess their need for further support.

AE1   Maintain and develop your knowledge, skills and competence.

With the introduction of the Qualification and Credit Framework (QCF), it is likely that the term 'National Occupational Standards' will change. At the time of writing, it is not clear what the new title will be, although it is known that some organisations will use the term 'QCF assessment units'.

Links to current NOS are provided at the start of each chapter; however, it should be noted that these are currently subject to review and it is recommended that you visit the Skills for Justice website to check the currency of all the NOS provided: www.skillsforjustice-nosfinder.com.

Introduction

This book has highlighted the crucially important role of the police in terms of interacting and working with victims. The purpose of this chapter is to expand on this and consider wider issues of victimisation, such as its consequences and how effective policing practice can help with victim recovery. It is important to reiterate that victims of crime are key players in the criminal justice process and, increasingly, 'customer satisfaction' is becoming an important aspect of police work. Victims are no longer just witnesses for extracting information but consumers of a service and this dramatically shifts the balance of power within the victim–police officer relationship. Indeed, some have argued that recent policy changes have realigned the CJS in favour of victims (Davies, 2004). In any case, there is little doubt that *one of the main functions of the police rests entirely upon the existence of crime victims* (Davies, 2004, p103). Police officers need victims for reporting crime, for securing arrest and for redressing social injustice.

Defining victims

REFLECTIVE TASK

Before reading about how we define victims, consider the following three questions.

- *How would you define a victim?*

- *What images come to mind when you think of a 'victim'?*

- *Why do we need to care about supporting victims?*

So how do we define victims and are there different types of victims? Spalek argues that there are four different definitions of victims.

1. *A person injured or killed as a result of an event or circumstance.*

2. *A person or thing harmed or destroyed in pursuit of an object or in gratification of a passion.*

3. *A prey; a dupe.*

4. *A living creature sacrificed to a deity or in a religious rite.*

(2006, p6)

Each of these definitions carries with it its own set of implications for how to construe a 'victim'. The first definition is perhaps the most common. The victim is blameless and the victimisation was outside their control. The second definition begins to blame the victim; they are the victim of their own pursuits. The third is a victim who has been preyed upon by a predator (for instance, a child groomed for sexual purposes) or who has been duped (perhaps an elderly person duped by a confidence trickster). The final definition has a wider set of implications. The etymology of the word 'victim' has been traced to those who are sacrificed. The implication with this definition is that the victim is construed as helpless and passive. However, feminists who have been influential in establishing a more 'critical' victimology are opposed to such passive victim definitions:

Not everyone who suffers victimisation likes to think of themselves or be called victim. Feminists . . . prefer to speak of survivors, for a number of reasons. 1) Using the term survivor makes clear the seriousness of rape as, often, a life-threatening attack. 2) Public perceptions are shaped by terminology and the word 'victim' has notions of passivity, even of helplessness . . . using the word 'victim' to describe women takes away our power.

(London Rape Crisis Centre, 1984, piv)

In victimology there are three main definitions of victims: direct, indirect and secondary. Direct victims are those who have been transgressed against in a way that contravenes the law (Dignan, 2005). In short, they are the identifiable victims. In terms of policing practice, we are more concerned with this type of victim. There is a wealth of statistics about the prevalence of direct victimisation, primarily from official statistics (e.g. police recorded data) and unofficial statistics (e.g. the British Crime Survey). There are various advantages and disadvantages in using these data sources, which will be expanded on in the next section.

Indirect victims are people who have either witnessed a crime and have been affected by it or are close family members or friends who are affected by the direct victim's victimisation (Goodey, 2005). Paul Rock (2008) refers to this as the 'ripple effect' in that it can be applied to many and varied individuals. Secondary victimisation refers to the (perhaps inadvertent) re-experiencing of the victimisation event through the criminal justice process. We will discuss in this chapter how police officers can minimise secondary victimisation through positive and effective interactions with victims.

A final important definition is of the 'ideal' victim. This victim is the stereotypical, and often fairy-tale, conceptualisation of the victim. The ideal victim is someone who is innocent, vulnerable, going about their business and is preyed upon by a big bad stranger (very much like Little Red Riding Hood) (Christie, 1986; Walklate, 2007). However, the ideal victim stereotype is a powerful image and can lead to bias when dealing with certain victims. The stereotype can lead people (particularly those with power) to label certain individuals as 'deserving' victims and so, by implication, label others as 'undeserving'. Police officers need to be especially mindful of this as victims are becoming more like 'consumers' of a service and so have expectations in terms of how they expect to be treated and how they expect you to respond. It is, then, important to realise that police officers are in a position of power and that the labelling of victims as deserving or undeserving can have consequences.

The prevalence of victimisation

In order to understand the psychological consequences and impact on victimisation we need to consider the prevalence and risk of victimisation. As mentioned previously, there are two main data sources we can use to investigate this: official and unofficial. The police have been officially recording crimes since 1957 and their data form a useful barometer for both public satisfaction with the police and the workloads of police forces. The police only record notifiable offences, that is, those offences that need notifying to the Home Office (e.g. theft, burglary, violence, drugs, criminal damage etc.). In 2009–10 the police recorded approximately 4.3 million offences, which represented around an 8 per cent decrease from the previous year. Property offences were the biggest group, although crimes against property have not risen, which we may have expected given that England was in a recession at that time.

There are, however, a number of limitations to police-recorded statistics. They only include offences reported to the police, yet evidence suggests that most crimes are not reported – these are referred to as the 'dark figure' of crime. Official statistics only include notifiable offences, excluding summary offences and those recorded by 'non-Home Office police forces', including the British Transport Police and the MoD Police (Newburn, 2007). Changes to Home Office counting rules means that some offences are not recorded, while some police forces engage in practices such as 'cuffing', which means that some crimes get recorded as 'non-crime'. It can also be noted that changes in police practice (e.g. police targets) mean that some crimes are upgraded or downgraded as offences (Newburn, 2007).

Since 2001 the British Crime Survey (BCS) has been conducted annually and has allowed for better estimates of crime (Jupp, 2006). The BCS is based on a sample of 40,000 respondents located in all force areas. The BCS is different from police-recorded data in a number of ways and has numerous advantages over 'official' statistics. The BCS asks people about their experiences of crime over the last 12 months, as well as asking respondents about their fear of crime, perceptions of crime and the impact of crime on victims. It has the advantage that respondents are self-reporting about their experiences of crime, so it captures offences that may not have been reported to the police. It is dependent on the victim's interpretation of the crime, rather than that of the police. The BCS thus allows an estimation of the gap between reported and unreported crime, and gives a more accurate snapshot of crime (Newburn, 2007). This gap is by no means inconsequential. In 2008–09 the BCS estimated around 10.7 million offences compared to 4.7 million reported to the police.

However, the BCS also has a number of limitations. Jupp (2006) argues that the BCS may not be sensitive enough to capture true incidences of domestic violence and sexual assault. It also excludes a number of crimes and people. For instance, it excludes those under 16 (although this is addressed in another survey), those in institutions, the homeless and other hard-to-reach groups; it excludes so-called 'victimless crimes', for example drug use/possession, underage sex and fraud (and corporate crime); and it excludes commercial or industrial victimisation (Newburn, 2007). The gap between recorded and actual crime is significant, but why would someone not want to report a crime?

Why might someone not report a crime?

There are, of course, many reasons why someone will not report a crime; for instance, it may be because they don't think it's worth it, they could be afraid of the repercussions, perhaps they can't face going to court, or perhaps they themselves are involved in criminal activity. However, one of the most consistent findings regarding whether people report crime and are satisfied with the level of service they receive is that it depends on the officer in a case. While this is perhaps more understandable for serious interpersonal crimes such as sexual assault or domestic partner violence, it also holds true for other crimes. A study that examined the satisfaction of burglary victims with the service they received from the police found that satisfaction was dependent to a large extent on the manner of the first officer on the scene and on keeping the victims informed of the outcome of the investigation (Coupe and Griffiths, 1999). This ties in with previous chapters of the book in that, once we form an impression of someone (or some group), it can be difficult to change it and police demeanour and interaction with victims is vitally important for victim satisfaction. Indeed, research has shown that a lack of communication between police and victims was strongly related to general victim dissatisfaction (Skogan, 2005).

The main determinants of victim satisfaction are being polite, helpful, fair and attentive (listening to what victims have to say and being willing to explain what is going on). Now we may say 'so what, who cares, why should we be bothered about victim satisfaction?' Well, the CJS is becoming much more victim-focused and so 'consumer' satisfaction is becoming more important. However, more than this procedural reason, it has been found that treating victims with respect and dignity can make police work much more effective. It has been found that, when treated fairly and respectfully, the public is much more likely to comply with requests from the police and also to obey the law. Positive experiences of the police influence how readily people report crimes, act as witnesses and identify offenders (Skogan, 2005). So, while it may not always be possible to obtain a positive outcome for the victim, it is *almost always possible to behave in ways that people experience as being fair* (Tyler, 2004, p89) and this determines people's views of the police.

REFLECTIVE TASK

- *Get a piece of paper and divide it into two; in one half write down some reasons why people would report a crime and on the other half write down why people may not report a crime.*

- *What could police officers do or be mindful of in order to improve the reporting of crime?*

The potential for non-reporting of crimes is increased for serious and violent interpersonal crimes such as rape and domestic/partner violence. These crimes involve more vulnerable victims, are more traumatic and emotional, and are likely to be committed by those known and/or trusted by the victim. As such, victims of these types of crime are more likely to blame themselves, to not report crimes or to not press charges. One of the main reasons for non-reporting is self-blame and feeling responsible for their own victimisation; another is because they feel the police would not be bothered. This is particularly the case when they are under the influence of alcohol at the time of the offence or when they perceive that their own actions led to them being sexually victimised (Fisher et al., 2003). Unfortunately, research has also shown that the CJS can blame the victim as well. For instance, Finch and Munro (2005) found that jurors consider many extra-legal factors when reaching a decision. These included stereotypical beliefs about intoxication, sexual assault and drug-facilitated rape. They also found a surprising level of condemnation and blame for victims. It is little wonder why few victims come forward and report such crimes.

The under-reporting of rape is a serious problem and serves to mask what is a huge social problem. Results from the National Crime Victimisation Survey in the USA have consistently shown that rape and sexual assault are among the most widely under-reported crimes, with only around 28.3 per cent reported to the police (Fisher et al., 2003). In the UK, Home Office figures suggest that, in 2008–09, 12,165 females (all ages) reported an offence of rape (Home Office, 2009). However, this only gives us part of the picture and we also need to consider 'unofficial' statistics. Amnesty International state that 167 women are raped every day in the UK; the BCS (2001) has reported that 1 in 20 women (aged between 16 and 59) in England and Wales have been the victim of rape. These are disturbing figures that dramatically exceed those present in official statistics (Blagden, et al., 2011). In Fisher et al.'s (2003) study of the reporting of sexual violence, they found that victims reported their victimisation to the police in the minority of cases (2.8 per cent), although in the majority of cases (79 per cent) they did disclose their victimisation to someone other than the police (generally a friend or family member).

One of the major problems, then, is the reluctance of victims to report rape to the police, principally because they do not think that the police will take it seriously or be bothered to investigate it, or for fear of being blamed (Westmarland, 2004). There is therefore a real need to address the stigma and not to dismiss cases that are complicated, for example a woman drinking in a private residence with a man late at night, making it difficult to establish whether consent was given or not (Fisher et al., 2003). It is important then, when an officer is dealing with such a case, that they offer as much support and guidance as possible.

There is also a similar pattern for domestic/intimate partner violence and similar reasons are given for non-reporting, including the violence being perceived as normal, shame and embarrassment, and fear of the consequences. While the reporting of such violence to the police is low, it has been found that the majority of victims (77 per cent) tell someone (this is similarly the case for rape victims) (Fanslow and Robinson, 2010). Police attitudes are also vital for the reporting of domestic/partner violence. Gracia et al. (2011) found that police attitudes corresponded with two different psychosocial profiles. One profile was described as 'conditional law enforcement' (depended on the willingness of the victim to report the offender) and the other as 'unconditional law enforcement' (regardless of the victim's willingness to press charges). There were significant differences between the two groups as to their attitudes towards partner violence. Police officers who had a preference for 'unconditional law enforcement' were higher on empathy scores, were less sexist and regarded partner violence as more serious than 'conditional law enforcement' police officers (Gracia et al., 2011). Those who were 'conditional law enforcement' police officers were more likely to see domestic/partner violence as an interpersonal problem rather than a criminal activity and would generally not want to be involved in domestic violence call-outs (Gracia et al., 2011).

Fear of crime

The fear of crime has been defined as *a rational or irrational state of alarm or anxiety engendered by the belief that one is in danger of criminal victimisation* (McLaughlin and Muncie, 2006, p164). However, before discussing this in relation to victims, it needs to be pointed out that ambiguities exist in defining fear of crime and that the phenomenon is complex. For example, what do we mean by rational and irrational fears (Farrall and Murray, 2008) and why are there differences in fear levels between race, gender and social class groups, and what do these reflect? Recently, the literature has begun to focus more on anxieties about crime. A study by Gray et al. (2011) examined the function of the fear of crime and generated three groups from their analysis: 'unworried'; 'dysfunctionally worried' (individuals who worried about crime and whose quality of life was also reduced by either their worries or their precautions or both); and 'functionally worried' (those worried about crime who took precautions that made them feel safer, but who judged their quality of life as unaffected by either their worries or their precautions). Gray et al.'s (2011) findings show that, while some people are worried, they can be motivated to take precautions that make them feel better while maintaining their quality of life. However, they did find more dysfunctionally worried individuals (27 per cent of the sample) whose quality of life was reduced by their worries and/or precautions. Interestingly, they also found that confidence in the police mediated some fears. For instance, those belonging to the 'unworried' and the 'functional' groups had higher levels of police confidence than the 'dysfunctional' group (Gray et al., 2011). This is an important finding as the fear of crime seems to be related to confidence in the police.

The fear of crime is sometimes referred to as a paradox in that, while crime has steadily reduced from the mid-1990s, the perception of crime is that it has risen (Gadd and Jefferson, 2007). People's fears may mean that they change their behaviour; they may become more anxious and this can have a deleterious impact on people's lives. This has led some to argue that the *fear of crime has become a major social and political problem, perhaps bigger than crime itself* (Gilchrist et al., 1998, p283). One of the most consistent findings in the fear of crime literature is that young men are at the highest risk of crime yet have the lowest fear. Women and elderly people have the highest fear but the lowest risk of crime. Fear of sexual violence and harassment from men underpins women's higher fears (Davies, 2007). Indeed, older women's fear of crime is three times higher than that of older men, which suggests that fear of crime is gendered as well as being related to age (Davies, 2007).

REFLECTIVE TASK

- *Think for a moment about your own worries of crime and the worries of those close to you. How worried would you say you are of crime?*

- *Do you think your fears (and those close to you) are rational or irrational? What would make a worry irrational?*

- *The British Crime Survey seeks to measure a person's fear of crime, so think how you would answer this question from the BCS: 'How safe do you feel walking alone in your neighbourhood at night?'*

- *What impact can high fear of crime have on a person?*

The psychological consequences of victimisation

There will always be a degree of subjectivity between how victims of crime react to being victimised and cope with such victimisation (Greve and Kappes, 2010). Differences in coping will depend on the type of crime and victimisation, but even within those types some will cope better than others. Norris and Kaniasty (1994) examined the differences between violent crime victims, property crime victims and non-victims as to psychological distress following crime victimisation. The study looked at symptoms of depression, anxiety, hostility, fear of crime and avoidance at three time periods (3 months, 9 months and 15 months). They found that, while crime victims' mental states improved after three- and nine-month periods, after such time they did not. The overall finding was that victims of violent crime remained more distressed than property crime victims, who were more distressed than non-victims.

The psychological consequences and impact of victimisation on crime victims can be numerous. For instance, interpersonal crimes (violence, sexual assaults etc.) have been found to cause emotional disturbances such as sleep and eating disorders, feelings of insecurity and fear, and low self-esteem. Table 6.1 summarises some of the psychological, behavioural and affective consequences of criminal victimisation.

Table 6.1 Psychological, behavioural and affective consequences of criminal victimisation

Type of consequence	Effects
Psychological	Cognitive meaning shattered (can't make sense of things; becomes distrusting and withdrawn)
	Low self-esteem
	Loss of control (feeling disempowered; loss of confidence)
	Self-blame
Emotional	Fear
	Anger
	Poor/problematic coping (e.g. hiding feelings)
Behavioural	Changes in lifestyle
	Withdrawal from social settings
Physical	Injury from offence
	Self-harm
	Suicide
Financial	Loss of earnings
	Costs of replacing items (particularly if uninsured)
	Excesses

Source: Adapted from Spalek (2006).

Spalek (2006) contends that the potential impact of victimisation is mediated by three factors:

- **pre-victimisation factors** – static or changeable variables such as age, marital status, employment, education or sexuality;

- **victimisation factors** – the situational context of the victimisation; for example, if an offence occurs in a believed 'safe' environment, such as at home or while in someone's care, the effect is greater;

- **post-victimisation factors** – support, intervention and so on can help victims cope.

The impact of victimisation can be compounded by a number of different factors including bereavement, relationship difficulties, poor health and pre-existing psychological problems. Considering the above three factors is important for policing and for delivering effective services to victims. There is individual difference in responding and coping with victimisation, as well as the social resources available to different victims, and so it is important to consider victimisation factors when interacting with victims, particularly those who are vulnerable.

'Vulnerable' groups have been the focus of sustained attention in victimology and have included women (particularly victims of rape and partner violence), elderly people and children. Elderly victims have been found to suffer longer from their victimisation (Greve and Kappes, 2010), so police interaction and the involvement of support services are crucial. Elderly people's responses to victimisation are usually compounded by pre-victimisation and victimisation factors. Many elderly people are victims in their own homes and are sometimes targeted because they are perceived as weak and as less likely to report their victimisation or to retaliate. They are also the group most likely to be socially isolated and excluded, so can fit the image of an 'ideal' victim (see page 73).

While research has shown that victims of a wide array of crimes can suffer from low self-esteem, anxiety and social withdrawal, this is exacerbated with vulnerable groups. One of the major psychological consequences of crime victimisation is associated with 'affect', which is, broadly speaking, the emotional consequences of crime. Such consequences include post-traumatic stress disorder (PTSD), depression, anxiety and suicide ideation (Ruback and Thompson, 2001). Perhaps the most widely researched affective consequence of victimisation is PTSD. When clinicians make a diagnosis of PTSD they usually refer to two sources: the *International Classification of Diseases, 10th Revision* (ICD-10) (WHO, 2007) or the *Diagnostic and Statistical Manual, 4th Edition, Text Revision* (DSM-IV-TR) (APA, 2000). The latter covers all mental health disorders for adults and children classified around five axes. The ICD-10 and DSM-IV-TR have similar conceptualisations of PTSD and both see it as a response to a stressful event or situation (either brief or long in duration) of an exceptionally threatening or catastrophic nature, which is likely to have an adverse effect on anyone.

The typical features of PTSD include repeated reliving of the trauma, intrusive memories, dreams or nightmares, obsessional thoughts and flashbacks, feelings of numbness, emotional detachment and distancing from others (APA, 2000; WHO, 2007). PTSD is also associated with, and found to be co-morbid with, depression, anxiety disorders and suicidal ideation (APA, 2000). PTSD has also been found to be associated with criminal victimisation (Ruback and Thompson, 2001; Kilpatrick and Acierno, 2003). For instance, it has been found that 32 per cent of rape victims suffered lifetime PTSD and that 12.4 per cent have current (within the past six months) PTSD. The rates of lifetime and current PTSD in physical assault were also high – 38.5 per cent and 17.8 per cent respectively. Overall, crime victims had higher rates of PTSD at 25.8 per cent compared to non-crime victims at 9.9 per cent (Kilpatrick and Acierno, 2003). Kilpatrick and Acierno (2003), in their review of the literature, found that lifetime PTSD in sexual assault victims ranges from 30 to 80 per cent. The psychological impact of rape, for example, cannot be overestimated, as it has been found that rape victims are six times more likely to develop PTSD when compared with women who have not been victims of rape. A study in the USA, using a large sample (n=1000), found that victims of physical and sexual assault reported significantly higher current PTSD than non-crime victims and victims of non-crime traumatic events (e.g. property damage from a house fire or natural disaster) (Ruback and Thompson, 2001).

One way in which the CJS has tried (to some extent) to address the psychological impact of victimisation and to help victims cope is through the 'victim personal statement' (VPS). Some argue that victims of crime are the forgotten voices of the CJS and that they should have a more active role in the criminal justice process (Wolhuter et al., 2009). In some ways the VPS provides an avenue for this and they were introduced in 2001 as a directive from the Victims Charter (1996). The Victims Charter began to shift the language in victim policy by introducing service standards (i.e. expectations) (Goodey, 2005). The VPS allows the victim an opportunity to tell the court how the crime has affected them (psycho-logically, emotionally, behaviourally, financially etc.). It is optional and is taken by the police, and it is argued that it can allow for a more democratic sentencing and help the victim recover from their ordeal (Goodey, 2005). However, there are also potential pitfalls in this process in that (even though the VPS is not admissible in court) it may invite prejudice or judgements based on emotion rather than reason (Myers and Greene, 2004).

PRACTICAL TASK

Read the BBC article 'Judge Told of Murder "Nightmare"' at http://news.bbc.co.uk/1/hi/wales/south_east/5385666.stm, and then watch the associated video clip – click on the link on the right-hand side that says 'There's no short cut through these cruel emotions'. Then consider the following.

- *What issues does allowing victims to address the court in such a way pose for the CJS?*

- *What are the positives and pitfalls of this procedure? Are you in favour of it and why?*

Coping with criminal victimisation

How do victims cope?

It is important for the CJS and thus for police officers that we have an understanding of how victims cope with their victimisation. As we have seen, victimisation has different effects both within and between victim types. One issue that is often overlooked with regard to victims' coping is stress. There is undoubtedly stress associated with being a victim of crime (particularly with violent and sexual crimes). However, what is usually overlooked is that victims still have the same everyday life stressors (e.g. relationships, work and family) as everyone else, but have extra stressors on top of all of these (Hill, 2009). Furthermore, the stress resulting from victimisation usually exacerbates life stressors, which can make it more difficult for victims of crime to cope with everyday life. Police officers should not underestimate their role in facilitating positive coping in crime victims.

Positive and negative coping

In the literature regarding the coping of victims there is generally reference made to positive (adaptive) coping and negative (maladaptive) coping. Criminal justice agencies such as the police can aid in promoting positive coping through relatively small contributions. For instance, one important factor related to positive coping in victims of crime is 'information seeking'. This may include information on support and advice being successfully communicated, being put into contact with relevant support groups, being updated about their case and the stages of the criminal justice process and having a sense of regaining control in their lives (Hill, 2009). Police officers, through sensitive early interactions with victims, can contribute to positive coping. Linked to the definitional section earlier in this chapter, how a person defines themselves could also affect how they cope with their victimisation. For example, individuals may initially embrace the definition 'victim' because it shows the person has been transgressed against and that they are a victim of wrongdoing. However, they may later shun this label and instead think of themselves as 'survivors', because this reflects recovery and fighting back and it implies strength (Hill, 2009). This shift in definition also implies a 'transformation' from a passive individual who has been transgressed against to someone who has overcome a negative traumatic life event and who has taken control and ownership of their life.

Some victims, however, find it difficult to adapt in positive ways. Negative coping in victims includes distancing oneself from others, withdrawing and isolating oneself, alcohol and substance misuse, self-harm and suicide ideation (McCart et al., 2010). These factors can be seen in our discussion of PTSD, which further emphasises that how one responds to a traumatic life event affects how one copes. But why might people differ in their responses to similar crimes?

Answering the above question is tricky and complicated, but how any of us deal with any event (good or bad) in our lives depends on what we bring with us to that event. In other words, we all are made up of different life experiences, and varying familial, cultural, socio-economic and educational backgrounds, all of which help us deal with and interpret future events or experiences. Individuals, then, differ in their internal frameworks, which can help buffer against negative life experiences and can help people react more positively to adversarial events. These internal networks are sometimes referred to as 'resilience'.

Resilience has been found to mediate the effects of crime victimisation and to minimise adverse psychological impairment and functioning through syndromes such as PTSD. Resilience is evident when a given event has little or no deleterious impact, perhaps because the individual is able to mobilise internal resources that existed pre-trauma, and it can promote positive coping. However, resilience is understood to be a multidimensional phenomenon (and not simply categorical, i.e. you either are or not resilient). For instance, a resilient survivor may be seriously impaired in one or more domains typically impacted by trauma and yet have remarkable strengths in others (Harvey, 2007). Resilience is also conceptualised as an active process by which individual survivors are able to access strengths in some domains in order to secure recovery in others (Harvey, 2007). It may be that individual coping resources are a key factor in successful coping responses (Greve and Kappes, 2010). Interestingly, resilience factors are a focus of psychotherapy with trauma survivors, that is, helping the individual recognise and mobilise their resilient capacities. However, it is important to note that most survivors will not seek out psychotherapy, so there is a need for an ecological framework that acknowledges *the importance of environmental interventions to foster wellness and enhance resilience among untreated trauma survivors and their communities* (Harvey, 2007, p16). This may be through public education campaigns, community schemes and educational programmes.

At the heart of such a framework appears to be the concept of 'moral repair', which is about the community helping the victim in restoring and creating trust and hope, and mending the harms caused at the hands of another (see, e.g., Walker, 2006). Indeed, beyond individual resources of resilience there is an emphasis that social support is effective for crime victims. However, while social support would seem an ideal platform to aid coping, such support for crime victims is low and generally only for specific crimes (e.g. violence against women). Helpers in such settings are generally ill-equipped to deal with victims' needs and are often not sensitive enough at recognising those needs. Relatedly, victims may not want or seek out social support because they may not want to talk about their crimes with others, and they may be experiencing shame and fear (Greve and Kappes, 2010). However, social support can help bolster the resilience of trauma survivors (Harvey, 2007) and it may be that police and community partnerships are a way of facilitating this support.

Finally, one of the most important aspects of coping with crime victimisation could be dependent on how much it is perceived to be threatening personal self-identity. This process is linked to attributional theory (see Chapter 3 of this book for a detailed discussion) and it may be down to how effectively an individual can 'neutralise' the consequences (direct and indirect) of a victimisation (Greve and Kappes, 2010). Such psychological processes (neutralising, positive illusions, self-deception) are not well integrated into victimological theory or well covered in the research. Indeed, self-deception (and its relation, denial) would usually be seen as a negative coping strategy and a sign of maladaptive coping. However, the distinction between adaptive and maladaptive coping is not always black and white, and the boundaries can become blurred (see, e.g., Hill, 2009).

In the psychological literature, denial and self-deception have been found to protect the self and to maintain self-esteem (Russell, 1993), thus performing an adaptive function. Furthermore, research suggests that honest self-appraisals are linked to depressive disorders (Seligman, 1975). As Cohen argues, *mental health, it turns out, depends not on being in touch with reality, but on illusion, self-deception and denial* (2001, p56). It may be for victims of crime that the use of neutralising techniques, positive illusions and attributional biases may be adaptive for some victims of crime (at least not inherently maladaptive in any case). It is contended that, through adjusting one's self-image, personal goals and values can help overcome the consequences of victimisation, so it is important we account for self-identity (Greve and Kappes, 2010).

PRACTICAL TASK

Read the article 'After I Was Raped' by Susan Brison at www.guardian.co.uk/books/ 2002/feb/06/society, which is an autobiographical account of being a victim of rape. This is a powerful article that provides personal insights into the psychological consequences of victimisation and recovery. Reflect on the article and on the importance of effective police work in helping victims report and recover from victimisation.

Effects of victimisation on indirect victims

So far we have only discussed the effects of criminal victimisation on direct victims (those who have been transgressed against), but how does the victimisation of someone affect indirect victims, for example family, friends and the wider community?

Indirect victims can face similar psychological consequences to the direct victim, including post-traumatic stress, depression, behavioural and affective problems, and social with-drawal. Indeed, the DSM-IV-TR definition of PTSD demonstrates that an individual does not have to experience a negative event directly. It is clear that PTSD can result from direct experience but also from *witnessing an event that involves death, injury, or a threat to the physical integrity of another person or learning about unexpected or violent death or injury experienced by a family member or other close associate* (APA, 2000, p465). Clearly, indirect victimisation can contribute to PTSD and research has shown that indirect traumatic experiences, such as being given the news that a loved one or close friend has been the victim of a violent death or injury, was as likely to produce long-lasting PTSD as direct victimisation (Ruback and Thompson, 2001). As you would have seen from the video clip in the task on page 80, losing a loved one through murder can have a devastating effect on the indirect victim and so, where possible, it is important they receive the support and advice they need.

Support for victims

As mentioned earlier, it has been found that social support can have a positive effect on victims' recovery and can help them cope with their victimisation. The 'post-victimisation factors', as discussed earlier, warn us that there is a crisis period immediately after victimisation that, if not addressed, could have irrevocable effects on the victim. It is at this crisis point that effective support is needed.

The current support for victims can be traced back to the 1960s and 1970s and the second wave of feminism, which was focused on structural inequalities (e.g. workplace, family and reproductive rights). The movements were to refocus and reorientate the CJS so that it favoured victims. It was largely because of the increase in victim visibility, which resulted in a greater recognition of vulnerable groups (particularly women who suffer from domestic and sexual abuse), that rights-based victims' movements started to occur (Blake et al., 2010). Victim support services are dependent on voluntarism and most could not survive without volunteers. Although there are differences between the agencies in terms of purpose and funding, most share similar philosophies in that they are about empowering the victim, encouraging them to think positively and to regain control in their lives (Davies, 2007).

The early 1970s saw the establishment of three main charitable support services: Victim Support, Rape Crisis and Women's Aid. Victim Support is the definitive voice for victims and the victim experience and is heavily funded by the government (approximately £230 million) (Rock, 2008). It provides services to approximately 1.7 million victims, of whom 1.4 million are from police referrals. It employs around 1,500 staff and 10,000 volunteers. However, it is not without its critics. Victim Support is a charity and yet survives because of heavy government funding while other services struggle financially to stay open. Goodey (2005) criticises Victim Support for not being 'apolitical' as it is not a neutral organisation. It is, then, a conservative promotion of victim-centred justice, but one done through consensus of government and criminal justice agencies (Goodey, 2005). There is a range of support services available for different types of victim and below are some of the groups and their purposes.

Table 6.2 Support groups and their purpose

Name of group	Support activity
Victim Support	Offers practical advice and assistance for crime victims and promotes victims' rights.
Witness Services (part of Victim Support)	Support services for witnesses throughout the courts in England and Wales.
Rape Crisis	Offers a variety of services including support and counselling, a 24-hour hotline, training and outreach work.
Women's Aid	A national domestic violence charity, campaigning for women and children.
SAMM	Provides support after murder and manslaughter.

PRACTICAL TASK

Choose two vulnerable victims (e.g. of hate crime, rape, domestic violence or elder victim abuse) and perform an internet search for support groups. Have a look at the different support groups available for each type of victim, and what they offer, and then consider the following.

- *How well do these support groups cater for victims' needs? Do they offer enough, or could they be offering more?*

- *Compare your two sets of support groups; is one better than the other? If so, in what ways could the other support group be improved?*

- *How well do you think the CJS and support groups address the needs of victims?*

The importance of effective police work

At the heart of this book is a reminder to students, those already doing police work or wanting to do police work, or those who work for a related criminal justice agency, that they are among the first people to interact with both offenders and victims and this carries with it great responsibility. The first interactions with victims are crucial and will come from you; you will shape their responses and their views of the police (and their likelihood of future reporting) and these can impact on their recovery. The central argument here is that much of police work is relational, so it is imperative that police officers reflect on their practice (see, e.g., Copley, 2011).

One of the main theoretical positions in victimology is 'positivist' victimology. This approach was shaped by the work of von Hentig (1948), who was concerned with the doer–sufferer relationship. He was concerned with the role of the victim and how they may contribute to or encourage their own victimisation (e.g. how they may provoke and create the situation leading to their victimisation). This early approach to victimology, however, was criticised as victim blaming (Rock, 2008). Nevertheless, this approach is still in use today, as we have seen in previous chapters when we discussed 'rape myths' and victim stereotyping; we still have a culture of victim blaming or of calling victims' characters into question.

There is a large body of research in psychology relevant to this approach to victimology and which helps us understand victim blaming more fully. Lerner (1980) argues that the 'just world hypothesis' is the need for people to believe that the world is a just place and that, by and large, people get what they deserve. It is suggested that people are motivated to see the world in this way, which can cause different responses to victimisation – it could lead to blaming victims, derogating their character, or helping them. Although a belief in a 'just world' is supposed to help maintain psychological well-being, the concern with justice can lead to victims being blamed. It is argued from this position that certain victims pose a threat to people's sense of justice (in that people may not always reap what they sow), so responses such as victim blaming or helping are attempts to restore a sense of justice (Hafer, 2000). Indeed, there are a number of studies that empirically demonstrate that the higher the belief in a just world, the more likely people are to engage in victimisation strategies (Hafer, 2000; Aguiar et al., 2008).

Responses resulting from a belief in a just world can be seen as a form of coping and may be an explanation of why certain victims (particularly rape and partner violence victims) are more likely to blame themselves. This can impact upon police work in a variety of ways. Let us take domestic violence as an example. Police attitudes regarding such an issue are crucial because they affect the victim and send clear messages to wider society concerning the level of social disapproval (or conversely tolerance) towards this kind of violence (Gracia et al., 2011). Just world beliefs and sexist beliefs have been found to influence police officers' views of women and the causes of partner violence. If police officers demonstrate or engage in practices that appear to blame or trivialise such victims, society will also condemn them.

One victimological position that can inform policing practice is 'critical' victimology. Critical victimology focuses on victims' lived realities as well as the way social structure shapes those realities (see, e.g., Mawby and Walklate, 1994). Critical victimology also focuses on the labelling process, how one acquires the label 'victim' and who has the power to label (e.g. the police). Critical victimology reminds us that defining people in a particular way (as deserving/undeserving) obscures the issue that victims belong to diverse groups, some of which may be structurally unequal or may hold relatively little power due to their social status. How a police officer then judges a victim (e.g. as deserving) will determine, to some extent, the level of service that victim gets, for example the level of support and advice.

CHAPTER SUMMARY

This chapter has focused on victims and victimology, and has considered the psychological consequence of victimisation for different crime victims (although with a focus on serious interpersonal crimes). The chapter has considered how one might define a victim and what that could mean for the victim (e.g. in terms of support and advice), the prevalence of victimisation (and why someone may not report a crime), the consequences of victimisation and the importance of the police in interacting with victims. This chapter thus supports the arguments from previous chapters in highlighting the key role the police have in shaping victims' experiences of the police, and in shaping the relationship the police have with the community and wider society (Skogan, 2005).

Research has shown that, when the police are viewed as fair, considerate and helpful, people are much more likely to obey the law, come forward as witnesses and press charges against offenders. Although our opinions of the police come from a variety of sources, people's direct experience is what ultimately shapes the experiences of crime victims. It must not be forgotten that the police do rely on the public to come forward to report and to apprehend criminals. We only have to look at the recent riots in London, and elsewhere in England, in August 2011 and look at the police appeals for help to capture criminals seen on CCTV to know that public cooperation is important to police work (see, e.g., *The Telegraph*, 2011).

One of the main aims of this chapter was to consider the consequences of victimisation and to examine how victims cope with it (both well and badly). Psychologists, academics and police officers have only recently started to think seriously about the consequences of victimisation and how victims cope (Greve and Kappes, 2010). However, the issue will become more important to all those involved with victims as the CJS keeps its focus on providing better services for victims.

REFERENCES

Aguiar, P, Vala, J, Correia, I and Pereira, C (2008) Justice in Our World and in That of Others: Belief in a just world and reactions to victims. *Social Justice Research*, 21(1): 50–68.

APA (American Psychiatric Association) (2000) *Diagnostic and Statistical Manual, 4th Edition, Text Revision* (DSM-IV-TR). Arlington, VA: American Psychiatric Publishing.

Blagden, N, Pemberton, S and Collier, C (in press) Rape of Adults, in Winder, B and Banyard, P (eds) *A Psychologist's Casebook of Crime: From arson to voyeurism*. London: Palgrave-Macmillan.

Blake, C, Sheldon, B and Williams, P (2010) *Policing and Criminal Justice.* Exeter: Learning Matters.

Christie, N (1986) The Ideal Victim, in Fattah, EA (ed.) *From Crime Policy to Victim Policy*. New York: St Martin's Press.

Cohen, S (2001) *States of Denial: Knowing about atrocities and suffering.* London: Polity Press.

Copley, S (2011) *Reflective Practice for Policing Students.* Exeter: Learning Matters.

Coupe, T and Griffiths, M (1999) The Influence of Police Actions on Victim Satisfaction in Burglary Investigation. *International Journal of the Sociology of Law*, 27: 413–31.

Davies, P (2004) Crime Victims and Public Policy, in Davies, P, Francis, P and Jupp, V (eds) *Victimisation: Theory, research and policy.* Basingstoke: Palgrave-Macmillan.

Davies, P (2007) Criminal (In)justice for Victims, in Davies, P, Francis, P and Greer, C (eds) *Victims, Crime and Society.* London: Sage.

Dignan, J (2005) *Understanding Victims and Restorative Justice.* Maidenhead: Open University.

Fanslow, J and Robinson, E (2010) Help-seeking Behaviours and Reasons for Help-seeking by a Representative Sample of Women Victims of Intimate Partner Violence in New Zealand. *Journal of Interpersonal Violence*, 25(5): 929–51.

Farrall, S and Murray, L (2008) Critical Voices in an Age of Anxiety: A reintroduction to the fear of crime, in Farrall, S and Murray, L, *Fear of Crime: Critical voices in an age of anxiety*. Abingdon: Routledge-Cavendish.

Finch, E and Munro, VE (2005) Juror Stereotypes in Blame Attribution in Rape Cases Involving Intoxicants. *British Journal of Criminology*, 45: 25–38.

Fisher, BS, Daigle, LE, Cullen, FT and Turner, MG (2003) Reporting Sexual Victimisation to the Police and Others: Results from a national-level study of college women. *Criminal Justice and Behavior*, 30(1): 6–38.

Gadd, D and Jefferson, T (2007) *Psychosocial Criminology.* London: Sage.

Gilchrist, E, Bannister, J, Ditton, J and Farrall, S (1998) Women and the 'Fear of Crime': Challenging the accepted stereotype. *British Journal of Criminology*, 38(2): 283–99.

Goodey, J (2005) *Victims and Victimology: Research, policy and practice.* Harlow: Longman.

Gracia, E, Garcia, F and Lila, M (2011) Police Attitudes Toward Policing Partner Violence Against Women: Do they correspond to different psychosocial profiles? *Journal of Interpersonal Violence*, 26(1): 189–207.

Gray, E, Jackson, J and Farrall, S (2011) Feelings and Functions in the Fear of Crime: Applying a new approach to victimisation insecurity. *British Journal of Criminology*, 51(1): 75–94.

Greve, W and Kappes, C (2010) Victims of Crime: Towards a psychological perspective, in Towl, GJ and Crighton, DA (eds) *Forensic Psychology.* Chichester: BPS Blackwell.

Hafer, CL (2000) Do Innocent Victims Threaten the Belief in a Just World? Evidence from a modified stroop task. *Journal of Personality and Social Psychology*, 79: 165–73.

Harvey, MR (2007) Towards an Ecological Understanding of Resilience in Trauma Survivors: Implications for theory, research and practice. *Journal of Aggression, Maltreatment and Trauma*, 14(1/2): 9–32.

Hill, JK (2009) *Working with Victims of Crime: A manual applying research to clinical practice*, 2nd edition. Ottawa: Department of Justice Canada.

Home Office (2009) *Crime in England and Wales 2008/09.* Available online at www.homeoffice.gov.uk/rds/pdfs09/hosb1109vol1.pdf (accessed 13 January 2009).

Jupp, V (2006) Victimisation Surveys, in McLaughlin, E and Muncie, J (eds) *The Sage Dictionary of Criminology*. London: Sage.

Kilpatrick, DG and Acierno, R (2003) Mental Health Needs of Crime Victims: Epidemiology and outcomes. *Journal of Traumatic Stress*, 16(2): 119–32.

Lerner, MJ (1980) *The Belief in a Just World: A fundamental delusion.* New York: Plenum Press.

London Rape Crisis Centre (1984) *Sexual violence: The reality for women*. London: The Women's Press.

Mawby, RI and Walklate, S. (1994) *Critical Victimology*. London: Sage.

McCart, MR, Smith, DW and Sawyer, GK (2010) Help Seeking Among Victims of Crime: A review of the empirical literature. *Journal of Traumatic Stress*, 23(2): 198–206.

McLaughlin, E and Muncie, J (2006) *The Sage Dictionary of Criminology*, 2nd edition. London: Sage.

Myers, B and Greene, E (2004) The Prejudicial Nature of Victim Impact Statements: Implications for capital sentencing policy. *Psychology, Public Policy, and Law*, 10: 492–515.

Norris, FH and Kaniasty, K (1994) Psychological Distress Following Criminal Victimisation in the General Public: Cross-sectional, longitudinal and prospective analyses. *Journal of Consulting and Clinical Psychology*, 62(1): 111–23.

Rock, P (2008) The Treatment of Victims in England and Wales. *Policing: A Journal of Policy and Practice*, 2(1): 110–19.

Ruback, RB and Thompson, MP (2001) *Social and Psychological Consequences of Violent Victimisation.* Thousand Oaks, CA: Sage.

Seligman, MEP (1975) *Helplessness: On depression, development & death*. San Francisco, CA: Freeman.

Skogan, WG (2005) Citizen Satisfaction with Police Encounters. *Police Quarterly*, 8(3): 298–321.

Spalek, B (2006) *Crime Victims: Theory, policy and practice.* Basingstoke: Palgrave-Macmillan.

Sprackman, P (2000) *Helping People Cope with Crime.* London: Hodder.

Telegraph, The (2011) London and England Riots: CCTV pictures of suspects are released by the police. Available online at www.telegraph.co.uk/news/picturegalleries/uknews/8690951/London-riots-CCTV-pictures-of-suspects-are-released-by-the-Metropolitan-Police.html?image=3 (accessed 1 September 2011).

Tyler, T (2004) Enhancing Police Legitimacy. *The Annals of the American Academy*, 593: 84–99.

von Hentig, H (1948) *The Criminal and his Victim: Studies in the sociobiology of crime*. Hamden, CT: Archon Books.

Walker, M (2006) *Moral Repair: Reconstructing moral relations after wrongdoing*. Cambridge: Cambridge University Press.

Walklate, S (2007) Men, Victims and Crime, in Davies, P, Francis, P and Greer, C (eds) *Victims, Crime and Society*. London: Sage.

Westmarland, N (2004) *Rape Law Reform in England and Wales.* School for Policy Studies Working Paper Series, Paper Number 7. Bristol: University of Bristol.

WHO (World Health Organization) (2007) *The ICD-10 Classification of Mental and Behavioral Disorders.* Geneva: World Health Organization.

Wolhuter, L, Olley, N and Denham, D (2009) *Victimology: Victimisation and victims' rights*. Abingdon: Routledge-Cavendish.

USEFUL WEBSITES

www.ageuk.org.uk – Age UK aims to improve later life for everyone through information and advice

www.cps.gov.uk/legal/v_to_z/victims_code_operational_guidance – *The Code of Practice for Victims of Crime*, Crown Prosecution Service Operational Guidance

www.fawcettsociety.org.uk – Fawcett Society, the UK's leading campaign for equality between women and men

www.rapecrisis.org.uk – Rape Crisis is a feminist organisation that promotes the needs of women and girls who have experienced sexual violence

www.samm.org.uk – SAMM is a national UK charity supporting families bereaved by murder and manslaughter

www.victimsupport.com – Victim Support is a national charity giving free and confidential help to victims of crime, witnesses, their family, friends and anyone else affected across England and Wales

www.victimsupport.org/~/media/Files/Policy%20and%20research/victims-code-of-practice.ashx – *The Code of Practice for Victims of Crime*, Criminal Justice System

7 Stress, burnout, coping and policing

CHAPTER OBJECTIVES

By the end of this chapter you should be able to:

- understand the concepts of stress and burnout and the impact they have for police officers and on police work;
- describe the main stressors in police work and the effective strategies for coping with stress;
- recognise the psychological symptoms of stress and burnout.

LINKS TO STANDARDS

This chapter provides opportunities for links with the following Skills for Justice, National Occupational Standards (NOS) for Policing and Law Enforcement 2008.

AE1   Maintain and develop your knowledge, skills and competence.
HA2   Manage your own resources and professional development.
HD6   Allocate and monitor the progress and quality of work in your area of responsibility.
HC6   Implement change.

With the introduction of the Qualification and Credit Framework (QCF), it is likely that the term 'National Occupational Standards' will change. At the time of writing, it is not clear what the new title will be, although it is known that some organisations will use the term 'QCF assessment units'.

Links to current NOS are provided at the start of each chapter; however, it should be noted that these are currently subject to review and it is recommended that you visit the Skills for Justice website to check the currency of all the NOS provided: www.skillsforjustice-nosfinder.com.

Introduction

So far in this book we have discussed how aspects of applied psychology can be effective in police work, from interviewing and interacting with victims and being mindful of stereotypes and judgements, to impression formation and the theories and motivations of offenders. The main consideration has been on the police officer's role as mediated by other people, that is, the effect they have on other people (victims, criminals, public). This chapter, however, is about the effects of policing on the police officer and will focus on the issues of stress and burnout. Most people who become police officers are excited about the challenge of the job, the variety of experiences on offer, dealing with different people and incidents and being a positive influence for the community. For many, becoming a police officer and joining the police force is the fulfilment of a life's ambition.

However, what happens when the challenges or demands of the job outstrip an officer's capacity to deal with them? For example, how does a variable shift (from busy to slow) affect officers, and how does exposure to threatening and unpredictable events affect them over a long period of time? These critical questions will be explored in this chapter, as will responses to stress, such as positive and negative coping. There is also consideration as to how coping strategies can be improved and how asking for help is, at times, necessary.

Stress

Stress has been defined as an unpleasant state of arousal in which people perceive the demands of an event as taxing or exceeding their ability to satisfy or alter those demands (Brehm et al., 1999). In essence, you are faced with an event or situation that you perceive as beyond your abilities to cope with at that time. Stress is common in humans and we will all experience it at different times in our lives and for different reasons. For example, you may be in a rush for an important meeting but are stuck in heavy traffic on the motorway; you may have too many deadlines to meet; you may be a student sitting your exams, the outcome of which will determine whether you go to university or get the degree result you want; or you may not have the money to pay all your bills. Stress is part of our daily lives and is a part of our daily vocabulary – 'I'm stressed out', the 'stress is getting to me' – sometimes followed by 'I can't cope.' Stress is increasingly recognised as a serious problem, so much so that there are helplines available to speak to someone if you are stressed and struggling to cope (see, e.g., www.anxietyuk.org.uk) and the internet has a number of useful resources to help identify and deal with stress.

A stressor is anything that causes stress and it is usually followed by efforts to reduce stress (coping). This stress and coping process (see Figure 7.1) is a back-and-forth transaction/relationship within the person's environment. When faced with a situation that is threatening or potentially stressful, our appraisal of that situation will determine how we will experience the stress and how we will cope with it (Brehm et al., 1999).

Figure 7.1 emphasises the personal and situational factors in someone's appraisal and ability to cope with a stressful event. Personal factors are the experiences the person has had beforehand and the situational factors refer to the environmental context. For instance, an appraisal or evaluation of something as stressful will be influenced by whether the stressor is novel (not experienced before) or predictable (experienced before); whether it is imminent (i.e. you don't have a lot of time to prepare for it) or not imminent; and its duration (i.e. how long the stressful event lasts) (Lazarus and Folkman, 1984). Thus, people will differ on their appraisal and coping of a stressful situation based on their subjective experiences and environment. This has led psychologists and researchers to try to better understand stress, and the sorts of situations that cause stress, in order for positive ways of coping to be identified.

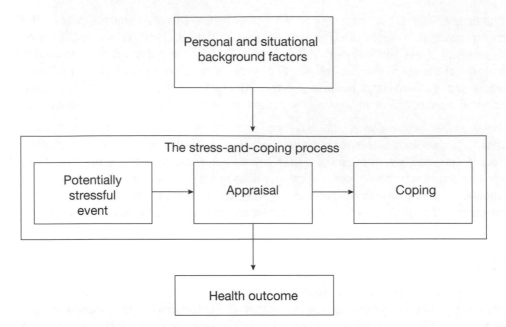

Figure 7.1 Personal and situational factors – adapted from Brehm et al. (1999)

Holmes and Rahe (1967) designed the 'social readjustment rating scale' (SRRS), which was designed to measure stress by evaluating how much readjustment different life events caused. The SRRS was essentially a checklist of 43 life events that were derived from clinical experience. The more stressful life events you face, the more readjustment and change you have to make and the more stressed you are. According to research by Holmes and Rahe (1967), the top ten stressful life events are:

1. death of spouse;

2. divorce;

3. imprisonment;

4. death of close family member;

5. major personal injury or illness;

6. marriage;

7. losing one's job;

8. pregnancy;

9. sexual difficulties;

10. addition of a new family member.

Holmes and Rahe (1967) make the point that it is change, positive or negative, that can cause stress. For instance, it can be noted that marriage and pregnancy are positive events, but each comes with great change and so require readjustment. Interestingly, it has been found that the experience of stressful events can make people susceptible to illness, as can the hassles and strains of everyday life. Negative life events have also been found to be associated with distress and physical illness (Brehm et al., 1999).

PRACTICAL TASK

How stressed are you?

- *Watch the NHS's short clip on coping with stress at www.nhs.uk/Livewell/workplace health/Pages/reducestress.aspx. Then, if you are comfortable, take their stress test.*

- *Then read the Health and Safety Executive (HSE) information on work-related stress at www.hse.gov.uk/stress/furtheradvice/wrs.htm. Look through the HSE's website and familiarise yourself with the signs of stress.*

Stress and policing

Stress is part of our everyday lives and most people will feel stressed at particular times in their lives. Policing, however, is often considered a highly stressful job as police officers are exposed to stressors that are unique to their working environment (Bradway, 2010), whether this is managing violence at football matches, dealing with town centres on Friday and Saturday nights, managing riots, interacting with victims or performing desk-based duties. The variability in the job, for example going from periods of intense working to quiet lulls, can also make policing stressful. Sewell (1983) devised a questionnaire called the Law Enforcement Critical Life Events Scale (LECLES). The scale consisted of 144 events that police officers would be likely to face at some point and officers were asked to rate them in terms of how stressful they perceived them to be. The events found to be most stressful were those that were violent or dangerous, e.g. violent death of a partner in the line of duty was ranked first, while dismissal, shooting someone in the line of duty and suicide of an officer who is a close friend were ranked second, third and fourth respectively. There were no significant differences between genders (Sewell, 1983). It is interesting to note that dismissal was ranked so highly and indicates that most officers want to keep their jobs. Events such as 'being passed over for promotion' and 'being investigated by internal affairs' were also ranked quite highly. These rankings may appear surprising and the research suggests that there are stressors within the policing occupation that may not be obvious to an outsider (Ainsworth, 2002).

It is interesting to note that research has shown that routine occupational stressors in police work (just as in other places of work), such as shift work, being passed over for promotion, feeling unfairly treated, and poor management and public attitudes appear more important contributors to stress and emotional maladjustment than the experience of traumatic stressors (Van Hasselt et al., 2008). So, while large critical incidences are stressful, police officers encounter more numerous smaller stressors that appear to have more of a deleterious effect on them (Van Hasselt et al., 2008). Perhaps one explanation for this is that large, critical incidences come with additional support (debriefings, counselling) and are probably expected by the officer, whereas the smaller stressors and internal bureaucracy do not come with support and are not expected. Gershon et al. (2009) similarly suggest that police stressors are associated with organisational issues, such as ineffective communication, rigid organisational structure, few opportunities for job progression, heavy and variable workloads, and shift patterns. Interestingly, research on police recruit 'dropouts' (those police recruits who resigned in the first 16 months of their police careers) has found that one of the main reasons for resignation was a conflict between the officers' ideal version of the police and the reality of policing practice (Haarr, 2005). This conflict highlights a discrepancy between what new recruits' expectations are versus the reality of police life, and this discrepancy can cause stress and eventually lead to someone leaving the force. Those who expect policing to be primarily about catching 'bad guys' may be surprised by the variability of police shift work and may also be surprised with how emotionally demanding the work can be. Couple this with bureaucratic procedures or target-focused management and this may lead to some officers becoming disillusioned and possibly more stressed.

The impact of police work on police officers

The nature of police work can itself be stressful; exposure to potentially dangerous situations, uncertainty about what you may face and the demands of the job can all contribute to feelings of stress. Exposure to and dealing with violent events and death have been found to be among the most stressful and studies focusing on police occupational trauma have shown the incidence of PTSD to be around 7 per cent in police populations (Rallings, 2002). This incidence rate has been found to be as high 46 per cent in shooting incidents (Rallings, 2002). We discussed PTSD in relation to victims of crime in Chapter 6 and it is important to recognise that police officers can suffer from the same symptoms. It is only recently that the police force has recognised this and the implications it has for the officer and the organisation. It used to be assumed that, due to experiencing emergency situations on a daily basis, police officers would not be as affected by them as people unused to experiencing such events. However, this premise has been found to be untrue and officers may indeed experience PTSD symptoms after a major incident (Ainsworth, 2002). Research has demonstrated that PTSD symptoms are present in police officers and that those with severe PTSD symptoms are three times more likely to have a metabolic syndrome, which can lead to cardiovascular disease (Violanti et al., 2006). This is supported by Bradway (2010), who documents that the self-reported incidence of cardiovascular disease was 31 per cent for law enforcement officers, as compared to 18.4 per cent in the general population. It has also been estimated that between 25 and 30 per cent of police officers have stress-based health problems, including high blood pressure, heart disease and gastrointestinal disorders (Van Hasselt et al., 2008).

It is now common to have debriefings following critical incidents and the police force can insist an officer sees a psychologist or counsellor. However, this does not guarantee that an officer will see a psychologist, as the 'macho' and tough ethos ingrained in police culture means that admitting to one's colleagues that you are seeking help would be difficult (Ainsworth, 2002). While the police have been described as 'emotional labourers' (see a discussion on this later in the chapter), showing or displaying such emotions is not compatible with some aspects of police culture.

Coping with stress

As can be noted thus far in this chapter, policing can be seen as a high-stress and high-strain occupation, and work-related stress in policing is related to negative outcomes such as depression, anti-social behaviour and problem drinking (Gershon et al., 2009). As noted previously, usually police stressors are associated with organisational issues rather than critical incidents. But what are the different ways of coping and how can coping strategies affect negative outcomes?

Lazarus and Folkman (1984) differentiated between two broad types of coping: problem-focused and emotion-focused. Problem-focused coping is where efforts are made to reduce stress by dealing actively with the problem and involves strategies such as planning or active coping, positive reinterpretation, information gathering and resolving conflicts. Emotion-focused coping is aimed at efforts to reduce emotional distress. It is about managing our emotional reaction to a stressful event rather than dealing with the problem (Folkman and Moskowitz, 2004). Strategies associated with this kind of coping include avoidant coping (i.e. not thinking about the problem and not dealing with it, e.g. you can't pay your credit card bill so you may pretend it's not a problem and not think about it in the hope it will go away – of course, it does not). Other strategies include denial, drinking and drug taking. It has been found that active coping (coming up with a strategy to deal with the problem) is highly effective in stress reduction; it gives people a sense of control and mastery over the stressor (Zeidner and Saklofske, 1996).

Although emotion-focused coping may bring some equilibrium to our emotional balance, a stressful event still requires a problem-solving aspect if it is to be adaptive (Zeidner and Saklofske, 1996). So, while emotion-focused coping could be adaptive initially, a reliance on it as a coping strategy is likely to lead to negative outcomes, for example depression and unresolved problems. For instance, denial is associated with emotion-focused coping, and Janoff-Bulman and Tanko (1987) conceptualise denial as a form of transition, which allows the self-concept to be protected and shielded from psychologically harmful information until the person is able to deal with the problem. Staying in denial of the problem is likely to lead to avoidant styles of coping, which can exacerbate a person's problems. Avoidant coping is generally regarded as a maladaptive form of coping in that it is associated with distress and negative consequences, and that typically it works against the person (primarily because you are not addressing the problem) (Zeidner and Saklofske, 1996). Coping research, broadly speaking, would suggest that it is better to deal with a stressful situation rather than avoid it (Billings and Moos, 1981).

As a police officer your style of coping could determine how stressful you find events and how such events affect you. Gershon et al. (2009) found that work stress in police officers was strongly associated with avoidant coping. Problem-based coping was found to help officers reduce stress and deal with the problem. Perhaps their most startling finding was that police officers who reported high work stress and who relied on avoidant coping mechanisms were more than 14 times more likely to report anxiety and more than 9 times more likely to report burnout than officers who did not use such a coping style (Gershon et al., 2009). The results of this study are clear, especially when we consider our earlier discussion on police stress and how high levels are associated with burnout, PTSD, anxiety and depression (Martinussen et al., 2007; Gershon et al., 2009). Gershon et al. (2009) argue that there are two ways to improve police officer stress. We can improve the coping mechanisms of officers and help develop an awareness of their coping styles or more work can be done in identifying and addressing modifiable stressors associated with policing. However, given the results of their study, it seems helping officers develop problem-focused coping strategies is a good step forward (Gershon et al., 2009).

There are effective ways to cope with and to reduce job-related stress so that it does not detrimentally affect your performance. One particularly good way of negating stress is through the effective use of supervision. In clinical practice settings (e.g. clinical psychology or psychotherapy), the use of supervision as a forum to reflect on practice and to discuss learning and job-related issues can reduce stress, and allow for more effective and creative ways of dealing with situations to be uncovered. Effective use of supervision and the receiving of 'good' supervision are vitally important, as a lack of support from superiors has been found to predict stress in police officers (see, e.g., Morash et al., 2008). It has been argued that good supervision and reflection start with a relationship of trust and transparency. This then leads to supervisees being able to talk about and reflect on incidences and issues, and to learn from them. This includes developing different strategies in dealing with similar incidents and issues in the future (Carroll, 2006). Reflective practice is becoming more popular in policing (see, e.g., Copley, 2011) and new police students will have to complete the Student Officer Learning and Assessment Portfolio (SOLAP) in order to demonstrate their skills as a police officer. Being able to reflect critically on incidents is one of the competencies student officers will need to demonstrate. Stress training has also been found to help reduce stress for those in the emergency services professions. Such training focuses on improving decision making under stress, controlling emotion and the fear of the unknown, coping with the unknown and building confidence (see, e.g., Sime, 2007).

As previously mentioned, there are numerous resources on the internet that can offer information and guidance about reducing stress and anxiety. Indeed, a search using the word 'stress' provides some valuable resources, such as the support group Anxiety.org, which has a helpline for those who are stressed and in need of someone to talk to. This process of talking with someone when stressed should not be underestimated and can dramatically help with coping with life's stressors. Readers of this chapter are directed to the 'Useful websites' section, which contains some great resources regarding stress, including links to the NHS and HSE.

PRACTICAL TASK

Reflect on this section and in the previous practical task. Now think about and write down some of the ways that police officers can cope positively with a traumatic event. Also consider the benefits of being mindful of one's coping style to policing practice.

Burnout and policing

Job burnout is a well-known phenomenon in many occupations, with its key defining characteristics being overwhelming exhaustion, feelings of frustration, anger and cynicism, and a sense of ineffectiveness and failure (Maslach and Goldberg, 1999). The impact of job burnout can be costly for the individual, and can result in ill health, psychological problems and general impairments in personal and social functioning (Maslach and Goldberg, 1998). Burnout is generally defined as a psychological syndrome consisting of three elements: 'emotional exhaustion' (feelings of being emotionally overextended and having depleted emotional resources); 'depersonalisation' (a negative, callous or excessively detached response to other people); and 'reduced personal accomplishment' (a decline in feelings of competence and productivity at work) (Maslach, 1993; Maslach and Goldberg, 1998). Undoubtedly, policing is a stressful job and exposure to threats of violence, attacks and different kinds of offences/offenders, as well as dealing with different victims and with human misery, contribute to stress. Police officers have to be mindful of becoming too 'stressed' and consequently becoming 'burned out'. There are some serious implications of this, as research has shown a relationship between burnout and the use of violence. Burnt-out male officers were found to use more violence than females and less emotionally exhausted officers, although it was depersonalisation that was the most important predictor of police violence (Kop et al., 1999). This has led Kop et al. to argue that *police personnel management should pay serious attention to burnout in general and depersonalisation among police officers in particular, in order to prevent escalating and violent behaviour* (1999, p338). A study looking at the relationship between exposure to violence and domestic violence in police families suggests that burnout may have a direct and indirect effect on spousal abuse (Johnson et al., 2005).

However, one of the striking findings regarding burnout and policing points to the positive aspects of policing. Indeed, research suggests that the overall level of burnout in police officers was not high when compared to other occupational groups (Kop et al., 1999, Martinussen et al., 2005). The level of emotional exhaustion has been found to be relatively low, with depersonalisation and personal accomplishment found to be comparable with other groups (Kop et al., 1999; Martinussen et al., 2005). It is important, then, to note the positive and rewarding elements of police work, such as variety and interest, a sense of reward and relationships with colleagues. While policing is a pressured job, it is not constant and so enables officers to have time to recuperate. It appears that many police officers can strike a balance between the stressful and rewarding aspects of their work (Kop et al., 1999). However, there is still a need for police organisations to be mindful of the effects of burnout, especially given that work–home pressures and lack of support have been found to be related to all three burnout dimensions (Martinussen et al., 2005). This is made all the more important when we consider the aforementioned findings of Johnson et al. (2005) regarding domestic violence. Martinussen et al. (2005) suggest that police organisations should try to reduce work–family pressures by identifying and improving working conditions that will make it easier for police officers to combine the two roles (parent/spouse and officer).

CASE STUDY

Jim is an experienced police officer and you have worked with him for a long period of time. You have recently noticed changes in his behaviour and you have begun to be concerned. One evening you are called to a domestic violence incident where both the man and woman are intoxicated and the man is being abusive. Jim takes exception to this and manhandles him to the ground. When the man gets up, Jim pushes him against the wall and you have to restrain him. Recently Jim has become more withdrawn, is indecisive with his decision making and frequently loses concentration. He seems more anxious than usual and is generally angry with people, both victims and criminals. You have also heard that he is spending excessive time in his local pub between shifts. When you ask him if he is all right, he replies sternly and says, 'Nothing's wrong, I'm fine, mind your own business.'

REFLECTIVE TASK

- *In the above case study, is Jim suffering from stress and/or burnout? What symptoms is he displaying? How is Jim coping and what coping style is he using? How could he change it?*
- *Think about how you could help Jim. What support could he receive?*

Poor coping, or when good cops go bad

Kroes once famously stated that *it is a rare police officer that does not show some negative personality change as a result of his years of police service* (1985, p21). This seemingly fatalist notion may be a slight dramatisation, particularly as research shows that most stress experienced by police officers is not from the content of the job, but instead comes from organisational processes and poor management. However, it does point to the issue that aspects of police work and job-related stress can contribute to some officers abandoning their policing role and engaging in criminal activity. Winter (2003) has termed this phenomenon 'slot rattling', the process whereby a person switches their outlook from one position to the next, that is, from law keeper to lawbreaker. This may happen due to a failure to adequately deal or cope with psychological or emotional issues. In such circumstances and under such stresses individuals can tighten or constrict their thinking so that people, events or situations are seen as 'black or white' or as 'either or'. For example, officers may construe people in extremes as either 'criminal' or 'police officer'. When under great stress, anxiety and conflict, it may be that police officers cannot see any alternatives and so resign themselves to becoming the other ('criminal') pole. Research on violent prisoners, for example, has found them to think in tight and constricted terms, meaning that they have few options available to them when in a situation of intrapersonal conflict (Winter, 2003).

Understanding police violence, anti-social behaviour and criminality is complex as it is caused by multiple internal and external factors. There has been a good deal of research on internal factors, and studies have focused on police personality, attitudes, values, stresses and strains (Ross, 2010). It has been found, as previously discussed, that police stress and poor coping are associated with anti-social behaviour, spousal abuse and violence in police officers. Kop et al. (1999) found a relationship between burnout and police violence. They hypothesise that this is due to two reasons: first, violence towards citizens is expected when they are viewed as impersonal objects (which can occur when the officer is suffering from depersonalisation); and, second, police officers who are stressed and emotionally exhausted will have fewer alternatives available to them to solve problems and conflicts in constructive ways (Kop et al., 1999). This links with Winter's (2003) contention that constricted thinking by officers, and hence a lack of options to approach a situation constructively, can lead to slot rattling. It also supports findings from the literature on police coping strategies, in that avoidant coping styles were found to be associated with stress, anxiety and burnout (Gershon et al., 2009). Furthermore, police officers who reported high levels of police stress were at an increased risk of a number of adverse health outcomes, including depression, burnout and PTSD.

REFLECTIVE TASK

Critically consider Kroes's (1985) argument (above) that it is a rare police officer that does not show some negative personality change as a result of his years of police service, *then think about the following.*

- *With reference to the literature discussed in this chapter, critically consider this argument and whether policing leads to negative personality change or other adverse psychological problems.*

- *In what ways can police officers avoid some of these adverse psychological problems and cope adaptively with the stressors they face in their job and daily lives?*

- *Do you think the stress and risk of burnout is greater for police officers than for people in other health or social professions, for example nurses or social workers? Why?*

Police officers as emotional labourers

While certain 'macho' elements of the police force may attempt to refute this, it could be argued that police officers are 'emotional labourers' because they have to engage proactively with their emotions as part of their daily role (Cornelius, 2000; Winter, 2003). 'Emotional labour' refers to how employees (in this case police officers) regulate their emotions in their work and the consequences of doing so (Van Gelderen et al., 2007). Emotional labour is particularly important for 'display rules', which state what emotions are appropriate for the individual to express in a given situation. As emotional labour involves rules, it can give rise to 'emotional dissonance', which has been linked to burnout and impaired psychological well-being (Van Gelderen et al., 2007). Emotional dissonance refers to the discrepancy between felt emotions and one's emotional display as required for the working context. For example, you may feel angry towards a man who has just beaten his wife, but you have to display a calm and professional manner. Similarly, you may be experiencing anger, but at the same time compassion and sympathy for the victim (Bakker and Heuven, 2006). Police officers, then, are required to manage their emotions, maintain neutral physical and facial expressions and be controlled. Some emotional experiences need to be supressed so that they can adequately deal with conflict situations, manipulation and aggression (Bakker and Heuven, 2006).

As police officers have to actively engage and manage their emotions, this can lead to emotional exhaustion and to burnout. This could also lead to 'constriction' of their thinking and mindset. When faced with incompatibles in their thinking (i.e. dissonance) people can restrict their perceptual field (i.e. black-and-white thinking), so that incompatibles are minimised and events are easier to predict (Winter, 2003). However, there are some serious consequences to this type of thinking. Think back to Chapter 3 about stereotypes and judgements – if police officers are constricted in their thinking, they may make stereotypical or prejudicial interpretations (consider the ramifications of making judgements such as all black hoodie-wearing young people are up to no good, or people from a certain area are all criminals). Constriction, or 'tight construing', limits a person viewing a situation from alternative positions and, as we have seen, this can lead to some police officers changing from law-upholding custodians into lawbreakers. Winter (2003) has suggested numerous ways to overcome discrepancies and constriction through the use of improved police training programmes (helping to elaborate officers' thinking), complementary assessment in police recruitment and therapeutic sessions for the stressed police officer.

REFLECTIVE TASK

- What do we mean when we say the police are 'emotional labourers'? What implications does this have for the traditional view of the police?

- Reflect on this section and think about what it means to engage with your emotions during your work. What impact could this have on you and what tensions might it cause?

C H A P T E R   S U M M A R Y

This chapter has considered the important issues of stress and burnout for police officers, and highlighted how stress can manifest itself in police officers. We have considered stress and how it is linked to coping strategies and processes, and have pointed to the potential hazards in using predominantly avoidant coping strategies in this line of work. The chapter highlighted that officers found organisational or structural factors as stressful, if not more so, than exposure to violent or traumatic events. We also considered the stressors involved in police work and their long-term effects on individuals. Although the chapter highlighted the problem of stress in policing, it should be noted that most police officers regard their role as positive and rewarding, with many officers dealing and coping with stress well.

There are, however, also significant numbers who report adverse psychological symptoms, so this chapter is an important one for police officers and the organisation. It is important for the organisation as it needs to take seriously issues of stress and burnout in individual officers, as their consequences can be severe for the individual officer, their families and wider society. It is important for individual officers to recognise that stress is a normal everyday process that everyone experiences, but that the nature of policing means that they are more likely to experience it. Officers need to be able to recognise the signs of stress and know that support is there through both formal and informal networks. Officers need to feel supported in seeking help, which should not be construed as weakness or failure. Good officers know their limits and capabilities, and know that, like all humans, they will feel stress. The important thing is how they deal and cope with that stress.

FURTHER READING

Gershon, RM, Barocas, B, Canton, AN, Li, X and Vlahov, D (2009) Mental, Physical and Behavioural Outcomes Associated with Perceived Work Stress in Police Officers. *Criminal Justice and Behavior*, 36(3): 275–89.

Toch, H (2002) *Stress in Policing*. Rockville, MD: National Criminal Justice Reference Services.

Winter, D (2003) Stress in Police Officers: A personal construct theory perspective, in Horley, J (ed.) *Personal Construct Perspectives on Forensic Psychology*. Hove: Brunner-Routledge.

Ainsworth, PB (2002) *Psychology and Policing.* Cullompton: Willan.

Bakker, AB and Heuven, E (2006) Emotional Dissonance, Burnout, and In-role Performance among Nurses and Police Officers. *International Journal of Stress Management*, 13(4): 423–40.

Billings, AG and Moos, RH (1981) The Role of Coping Resources in Attenuating the Stress of Life Events. *Journal of Behavioral Medicine*, 4: 139–57.

Bradway, J (2010) Gender Stress and Differences in Critical Life Events among Law Enforcement Officers. *Journal of Public Service eLearning*, 1(5): 1–22.

Brehm, SS, Kassin, SM and Fein, S (1999) *Social Psychology.* New York: Houghton Mifflin.

Carroll, M (2006) Key Issues in Coaching Psychology Supervision. *The Coaching Psychologist*, 2(1): 4–8.

Copley, S (2011) *Reflective Practice for Policing Students.* Exeter: Learning Matters.

Cornelius, N (2000) Difference, Inclusion, and Exclusion among 'Emotional Labourers': A search for meanings, in Fisher, JM and Cornelius, N (eds) *Challenging the Boundaries: PCP perspectives for the new millennium.* Farnborough: EPCA.

Folkman, S and Moskowitz, JT (2004) Coping: Pitfalls and promise. *Annual Review of Psychology*, 55: 745–74.

Gershon, RM, Barocas, B, Canton, AN, Li, X and Vlahov, D (2009) Mental, Physical and Behavioural Outcomes Associated with Perceived Work Stress in Police Officers. *Criminal Justice and Behaviour*, 36(3): 275–89.

Haarr, RN (2005) Factors Affecting the Decision of Police Recruits to 'Drop Out' of Police Work. *Police Quarterly*, 8(4): 431–53.

Holmes, TH and Rahe, RH (1967) The Social Readjustment Scale. *Journal of Psychosomatic Research*, 11(2): 213–18.

Janoff-Bulman, R and Timko, C (1987) Coping with Traumatic Life Events: The role of denial in light of people's assumptive worlds, in Snyder, CR and Ford, C (eds) *Coping with Negative Life Events: Clinical and social psychological perspectives.* New York: Plenum.

Johnson, LB, Todd, M and Subramanian, G (2005) Violence in Police Families: Work–family spillover. *Journal of Family Violence*, 20: 3–12.

Kop, N, Euwema, M and Schaufeli, W (1999) Burnout, Job stress and Violent Behaviour among Dutch Police Officers. *Work & Stress*, 13(4): 326–40.

Kroes, WH (1985) *Society's Victim: The police officer.* Springfield, IL: Thomas.

Lazarus, RS and Folkman, S (1984) *Stress, Appraisal and Coping.* New York: Springer.

Martinussen, M, Richardson, AM and Burke, RJ (2005) Job Demands, Job Resources, and Burnout among Police Officers. *Journal of Criminal Justice*, 35: 239–49.

Maslach, C (1993) Burnout: A multidimensional perspective, in Schaufei, C, Maslach, C and Marek, T (eds) *Professional Burnout: Recent developments in theory and research.* Washington, DC: Taylor and Francis.

Maslach, C and Goldberg, J (1998) Prevention of Burnout: New perspectives. *Applied & Preventative Psychology*, 7: 63–74.

Morash, M, Kwak, D-H, Lee, CH, Cho, SH and Moon, B (2008) Stressors, Coping and Strategies, and Police Stress in South Korea. *Journal of Criminal Justice*, 36(3): 231–9.

Rallings, M (2002) The Impact of Offending on Police Officers. *Issues in Forensic Psychology*, 3: 20–40.

Ross, J (2010) *Policing Issues: Challenges and controversies.* London: Jones & Bartlett Learning International.

Sewell, JD (1983) The Development of a Critical Life Events Scale for Law Enforcement. *Journal of Police Science and Administration*, 11(1): 109–16.

Sime, JA (2007) Designing Emergency Response Training: Seven ways to reduce stress, in *Proceedings of the IADIS International Conference on Cognition and Exploratory Learning in Digital Age*. Online at www.iadis.net/dl/final_uploads/200714L006.pdf (accessed 30 November 2011).

Van Gelderen, B, Heuven, E, Van Veldhoven, M, Zeelenberg, M and Croon, M (2007) Psychological Strain and Emotional Labour among Police Officers: A diary study. *Journal of Vocational Behaviour*, 71: 446–59.

Van Hasselt, VB, Sheehan, DC, Malcolm, AS, Sellers, AH, Baker, MT and Couwels, J (2008) The Law Enforcement Officer Stress Survey (LEOSS): Evaluation of psychometric properties. *Behaviour Modification*, 32(1): 133–51.

Violanti, JM, Fekedulegn, D, Hartley, TA, Andrew, ME, Charles, LE, Mnatsakanova, A and Burchfiel, CM (2006) Police Trauma and Cardiovascular Disease: Association between PTSD symptoms and metabolic syndrome. *International Journal of Emergency Mental Health*, 8(4): 227–37.

Winter, D (2003) Stress in Police Officers: A personal construct theory perspective, in Horley, J (ed.) *Personal Construct Perspectives on Forensic Psychology*. Hove: Brunner-Routledge.

Zeidner, M and Saklofske, DS (1996) Adaptive and Maladaptive Coping, in Zeidner, M and Endler, NS (eds) *Handbook of Coping*. New York: Wiley.

USEFUL WEBSITES

http://helpguide.org/mental/stress_signs.htm – Helpguide.org's Understanding Stress

www.anxietyuk.org.uk/about-anxiety/stress/?gclid=CMDe6KmF8KoCFcUMtAodKRNJOQ – Anxiety UK, information on stress

www.bbc.co.uk/health/emotional_health/mental_health/mind_stress.shtml – BBC Health information on the consequences of too much stress, and links to useful organisations

www.greenmedicolegal.com/PTSDPOLICE.pdf – A report on PTSD in UK police officers by Ben Green

www.hse.gov.uk/stress – Health and Safety Executive, help for work-related stress

www.nhs.uk/Conditions/Stress/Pages/Introduction.aspx – NHS Choices, information on managing stress

www.nhs.uk/Livewell/workplacehealth/Pages/reducestress.aspx – NHS Choices, stress test and stress checklist

www.npia.police.uk – National Policing Improvement Agency

www.skillsforjustice.com/What-we-do/For-individuals/Careers/Careers-Choices/Policing-Law-Enforcement – Skills for Justice, Policing & Law Enforcement

www.stress.org.uk – Stress Management Society

8 Conclusion

This book has examined how psychology can be applied to the many and varied aspects of police work. It has drawn on a range of psychological theories, concepts and research to explore the relevance and influence of psychology in modern-day policing. The book has focused on the relational aspects of policing, such as the importance of effective interpersonal and communication skills. These are becoming more and more important for policing due to 'customer satisfaction' being an outcome of police performance. The book has also focused on psychological theories of criminal behaviour, stereotyping, investigative psychology, victims and staff burnout. It has demonstrated how psychological principles can be applied to these areas and how these can be beneficial to police work.

Although the relationship between psychology and policing has been, at times, an uneasy one, with scepticism from both sides, there is now a mutual respect and recognition that each contributes to the other's discipline and learning. In recent times there has been a much more collaborative partnership between psychology and policing, developing over a comparatively short period of time. Indeed, before the 1960s there was very little interaction between psychology or psychological services and law enforcement agencies. The relationship, then, has gone from being estranged, or even non-existent, to one that is now flourishing and is universal in many aspects of policing practice (Weiss and Inwald, 2010). This relationship is likely to remain a blossoming one as the policing agenda remains focused around community and public safety (Weiss and Inwald, 2010).

The focus of the book

Chapter 2 outlined some of the most prominent psychological theories explaining criminal behaviour. This is beneficial as it can help with effective and more informed decision making, as well as help guard against making stereotypical or oversimplistic interpretations of people. The SARA (scanning, analysis, response and assessment) model is frequently used in police training (particularly with regard to community-led and problem-orientated policing), so a sound understanding of psychological theories could help with an appropriate 'response' or action from an officer (see, e.g., Haar, 2001). Currently, police officers are involved in their communities with models of policing requiring officers to participate in, collaborate with and promote the communities they serve (Haar, 2001). This means that effective decision-making, communication and interpersonal skills are necessary for a range of police practices (this has been stressed at numerous points in this volume, but see Chapters 4 and 6 especially).

Chapter 3 focused on the crucial issue of stereotyping and biased attributions in policing. The Scarman and Macpherson reports highlighted that aspects of the force were institutionally racist, and a BBC documentary (*The Secret Policeman*, 2006) again illuminated the issue of racism within the police. It goes without saying that this is wholly unacceptable, but students, officers and those wanting to work in the police need to be aware of their prejudices and to be mindful of the dangers of stereotyping individuals. This is of the utmost importance, as it is crucial that police officers are not biased in their judgements or they run the risk of discriminatory practice.

Some recent research has found that, while policing racist incidents was taken seriously at a senior management level, at an operational level it was not. There was a tendency for operational staff to view black and minority ethnic communities as problematic or criminogenic. These prevailing attitudes are likely to have a deleterious impact on policing practice and could result in the poor policing of racially motivated crime (Patel, 2011). The study highlighted that racial stereotypes and other negative attitudes are hard to remove from official policing practice (Patel, 2011). Thus, this chapter focused on how stereotypes and biased thinking are formed, and underlined some of the psychological principles that can drive stereotypical thinking.

Chapter 4 focused on effective interpersonal and communication skills and the importance of these in policing practice. The chapter described key issues relating to interviewing both victims and offenders. Chapter 5 discussed the different approaches to offender profiling and the merits and pitfalls of the main approaches. This chapter also highlighted the benefits of profiling for policing practice. Chapter 6 examined the relationship between victims and the police, and how crucial this relationship is for victims' experiences of the CJS. The chapter also focused on the consequences of victimisation and particularly the experience of PTSD in crime victims. Finally, Chapter 7 focused on burnout and stress in police officers. The chapter pointed out that, while most police officers are positive about their jobs, there are stresses inherent in policing that can cause additional job-related stress and this can spill over into officers' private lives. The chapter stressed the importance of self-care and also the resources that are open to officers both within the force and beyond.

Future directions

We have seen in this book that insights from psychological research, perspectives and theory can inform various aspects of police work from interviewing and interacting with victims and suspects to informing investigation. Indeed, psychology can be applied to many aspects of the criminal justice process (e.g. courts), as well as law enforcement. While psychology and psychologists have had an increasing impact on these processes in recent times, much more still needs to be done. There still exists a major problem in that investigators, lawyers, judges and others working in the CJS receive little or no background in psychological theory as part of their training and have little understanding of basic psychological processes (Williamson, 2007). In some ways this lack of understanding can be exemplified in the case of expert witness testimony. Indeed, the courts have been less than enthusiastic about psychologists appearing as experts and the case of *R* v. *Turner* (1975) meant that psychological knowledge was effectively seen as comprising 'common knowledge and experience'. Thus, psychologists were limited in only being able to provide testimony on the mental abnormality of an individual. It was not until the case of *R* v. *Emery* (1993) that psychological evidence was held as being complex and outside public knowledge (Kapardis, 2010).

Clearly, then, psychology has some way to go and still more to offer to both policing and criminal justice. In the USA, 'police psychology' is a much more recognised discipline, with psychologists involved in the screening and selection of officers, police training and counselling. Furthermore, they provide assistance in investigations and other areas of police work, such as interviewing and hostage negotiation (Bartol and Bartol, 2011). In the UK, psychologists still play a relatively minor role in aspects of policing, with perhaps the best strides being made on the investigation side. However, as Williamson (2007) notes, one challenge facing psychology is to convince investigators, lawyers and judges that they need a better understanding of psychological processes in crime and criminal behaviour. One of the practical benefits psychology has to offer investigators is through investigative psychology. However, if psychology is to go beyond traditional offender profiling it needs to establish a firm scientific base and this requires collecting data, databases, networks and analytical tools that will enable profiling to progress from deductive investigations to inductive and knowledge-based investigations (Williamson, 2007).

Finally, to echo the sentiments of Ainsworth (2002), it is hoped that students, police officers and those wanting to pursue careers in policing who have read through this book are now more convinced of the utility and value that psychology can offer policing and the contribution it can make in this area. Hopefully, it has been made clear that psychology plays a pivotal role in policing, even if that role is not always explicitly recognised.

CHAPTER SUMMARY

This book has highlighted that the majority of police work involves others – people to report crimes, the public to act as witnesses, and victims to support and advise. Much of the work police officers do is, then, relational and interactional – it involves other people. Thus, this book has focused on key issues relating to interpersonal skills and interpersonal effectiveness.

While the relationship between psychology and policing has strengthened, there is room for development, particularly in terms of training and recruitment. In the UK, psychology and psychologists are not as actively involved in police training as they are in the USA. There, psychologists are involved in many aspects of training, recruitment and assessment (and many also offer a counselling service) (Weiss and Inwald, 2010). While police forces in the UK are yet to embrace fully the potential benefits of psychology (and perhaps law enforcement agencies never will fully embrace it – see White and Honig, 1995), this book has hopefully highlighted that psychology has much to offer policing practice and that it is helpful and adds value to many aspects of policing.

REFERENCES

Ainsworth, PB (2002) Psychology and Policing. Cullompton: Willan.

Bartol, CR and Bartol, AM (2011) *Introduction to Forensic Psychology.* London: Sage.

Haar, RN (2001) The Making of a Community Police Officer: The impact of basic training and occupational socialization of police recruits. *Police Quarterly*, 4(4): 402–33.

Kapardis, A (2010) *Psychology and the Law: A critical introduction.* Cambridge: Cambridge University Press.

Patel, TG (2011) Policing Racist Incidents: Views and experiences of officers within the Police Service of Northern Ireland. *The Journal of Criminal Justice*, 1(2): 1–16.

Weiss, PA and Inwald, R (2010) A Brief History of Personality Assessment in Police Psychology, in Weiss, PA (ed.) *Personality Assessment in Police Psychology: A 21st century perspective.* Springfield, IL: Charles C Thomas.

White, EK and Honig, AL (1995) The Role of the Police Psychologist in Training, in Jurke, MI and Scrivener, EM (eds) *Police Psychology in the 21st Century*. Hillsdale, NJ: LEA.

Williamson, T (2007) Psychology and Criminal Investigation, in Newburn, T, Williamson, T and Wright, A (eds) *Handbook of Criminal Investigation*. Cullompton: Willan.

Index